MATH GAMES GRADE 6

By

JOYCE A. STULGIS-BLALOCK

ISBN 1-58037-275-9

Printing No. CD-404002

Mark Twain Media, Inc., Publishers
Distributed by Carson-Dellosa Publishing Company, Inc.

Table of Contents

Introduction to the Teacher

These math games were developed over the past several years. Students in many grade levels have tried them and have really enjoyed playing them. The games were designed to reinforce the National Council of Teachers of Mathematics (NCTM) Standards. The standards that pertain to each game are noted at the top of each page.

The games are unique, because they incorporate several skills. They are not only math "skills" games, but are also games of "strategy." The students must have good math knowledge, but they must also be thinking of where they want to move in the answer boxes with their next solution to achieve three boxes in a row.

Here are some ways in which the games may be played:

1. Students can be given a page as a morning practice sheet.
2. They can play the games as a race, to see who finishes first.
3. The pages can be used as test preparation.
4. They can be played with partners or in teams of three.
5. If the teacher makes a transparency of a game, it can be played with competing teams within the class.
   (More detailed directions follow this page.)

I hope this book will help you and your students.

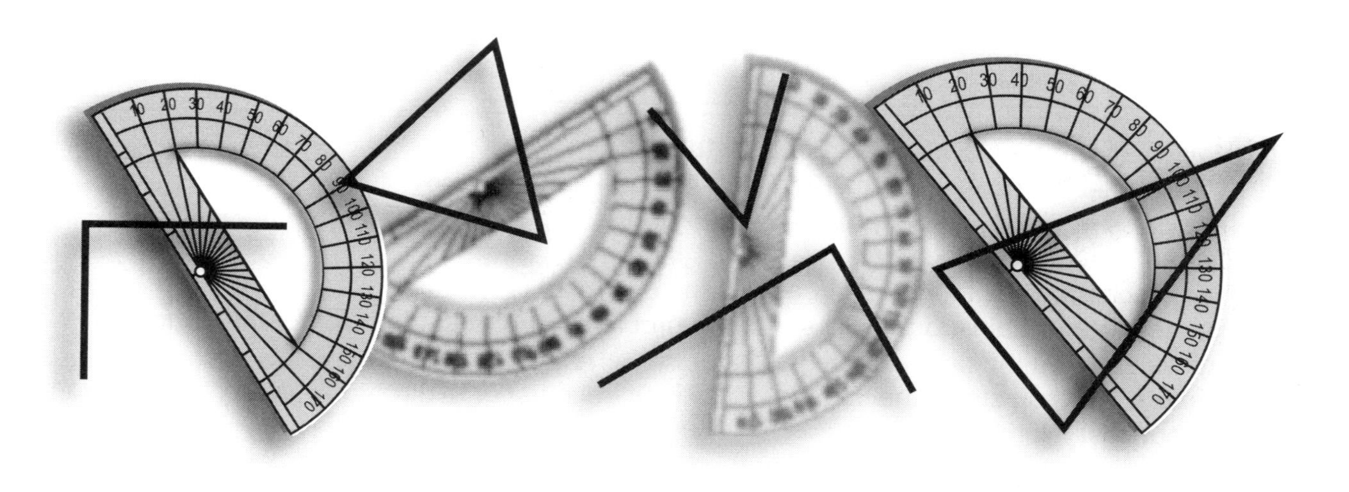

Directions for Playing Math Games

To play the games individually as a review, a learning exercise, or as a morning warm-up exercise:

1. First, the teacher chooses the skill he/she wants the students to practice.
2. Copies of the chosen game are made for each student.
3. The games are passed out facedown on the students' desks.
4. When the teacher says, "Go," the students turn over the game, and they begin to match answers in the boxes on the right side of the page to the problems listed on the left side of the page.
5. They write the number of the problem in the box that has the correct answer. They must then cross out the number of the problem they have solved. When the whole class has finished, the teacher calls out the answers, and the students correct their own work, or they can exchange with a partner, and the partner can correct the game.

To play the games in teams of 2 or 3 players:

1. The teacher chooses the skill the students need to practice.
2. Copies of the chosen game are made for every two or three students.
3. The class is divided into teams of two or three students, and it is determined who will go first, second, and third.
4. The teacher passes out the games facedown, one game per team.
5. When the teacher says, "Go," the students turn over the game.
6. The student who goes first chooses any problem on the left side of the page to complete. If the answer is correct, or the other player(s) agree with the answer, the first player puts his/her initials and the problem number in the answer box and crosses out the question. If the answer is NOT correct, that student loses a turn. Right or wrong, the game paper passes to student number two. After student number two finishes, the game passes to student number three, and so the game continues.
7. The person who gets any three answer boxes in a row wins. Each answer box can only be used one time for a win. The game can continue until all of the boxes are claimed or until a win is no longer possible.

To play the games as a whole-class activity:

1. The teacher chooses the game and then makes a transparency of it.
2. The class is divided into teams of three or four students each. Each team should be represented by a name or number.
3. The teacher places the transparency on the overhead projector.
4. The teacher explains to the class that the problems are on the left side of the page, and the answers are on the right side of the page.
5. The teacher then states that he/she will call out the number of a problem; for example, he/she announces: "Number 5."
6. The first person to raise his/her hand, or the person the teacher calls upon, will state the answer to Number 5. If it is correct, then that team claims that answer box, and the team's name or number and the problem number is placed in that box. The teacher then crosses out the problem that has been solved, so the students will not attempt to solve it again.
7. The winner is either the team with the most boxes or the team that claims three boxes in a row; the teacher can make the choice.

NCTM Standard: Algebra – use symbolic algebra to represent problems; represent the idea of an unknown in expressions and equations

Dance Away With Algebraic Expressions

Below are algebraic expressions. Find the definition of each expression in the boxes to the right.

1. $a + 5 =$
2. $5 + a =$
3. $n + 4 =$
4. $n + 3 =$
5. $a + 6 =$
6. $n + 6 =$
7. $4 + n =$
8. $3 + n =$
9. $6 + a =$
10. $n - 5 =$
11. $5 - a =$
12. $6 - a =$
13. $n - 6 =$
14. $a - 6 =$
15. $5 - n =$

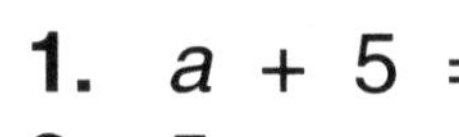

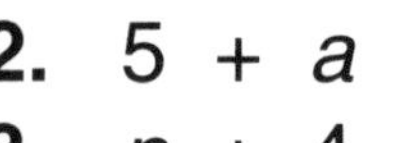

six added to *n*	5 minus the quantity *n*	the quantity *a* added to 6
a less than 5	5 more than *a*	*n*, take away 6
3 more than *n*	*a* taken away from 6	4 more than *n*
a more than 5	5 less than *n*	the quantity *n* added to 4
the quantity *n* added to 3	6 added to *a*	*a* minus the quantity 6

NCTM Standard: Number and Operations – compute fluently and make reasonable estimates

Glide Through Algebraic Equations

Solve the equations below, and find the value for the unknown in the boxes to the right.

1. $0.369 \div n = 0.123$
2. $0.205 \div a = 0.041$
3. $0.50 \div y = 0.05$
4. $0.568 \div n = 0.71$
5. $0.639 \div y = 0.071$
6. $0.357 \div n = 0.51$
7. $0.306 \div a = 0.051$
8. $0.546 \div m = 0.91$
9. $0.637 \div n = 0.091$
10. $0.526 \div y = 0.263$
11. $0.789 \div n = 0.0263$
12. $0.32 \div m = 0.016$
13. $0.50 \div n = 5$
14. $0.60 \div y = 0.05$
15. $0.160 \div m = 0.004$
16. $0.250 \div a = 0.005$

12	0.8	40	10
2	30	50	5
0.6	6	20	7
3	0.1	0.7	9

NCTM Standard: Algebra – use symbolic algebra to represent problems; determine value of unknown in expressions and equations

Hook Algebraic Unknowns

Solve the equations below by finding the value of the unknown. Then find the answer in the boxes to the right.

1. $45 = 5n - 5$
2. $15 = 2a + 9$
3. $13 = 3p + 1$
4. $16 = 3m + 1$
5. $18 = 5n + 3$
6. $38 = 3p + 2$
7. $65 = 5a + 5$
8. $37 = 4m + 1$
9. $12 = 2n + 2$
10. $32 = 4a + 4$
11. $29 = 5p - 11$
12. $25 = 3m + 19$
13. $27 = 4n + 3$
14. $92 = 3a + 2$
15. $23 = 4p + 11$
16. $9 = 5m + 4$

$m = 1$	$n = 10$	$p = 3$	$m = 2$
$p = 12$	$a = 30$	$a = 3$	$m = 9$
$a = 12$	$p = 4$	$n = 5$	$p = 8$
$n = 3$	$n = 6$	$m = 5$	$a = 7$

NCTM Standard: Algebra – represent mathematical situations using algebraic symbols

Zip Away With Algebraic Expressions

Read each description below, and find the matching expression in the boxes to the right.

1. 5 more than the quantity a
2. 3 less than the quantity n
3. 6 added to the quantity z
4. 5 less than the quantity n
5. 6 less than the quantity n
6. 5 more than the quantity n
7. n less than 4
8. 4 divided by the quantity n
9. the quantity n divided by 4
10. 6 less than the quantity a
11. the quantity a more than 6
12. 12 more than the quantity n
13. 12 divided by the quantity a
14. 6 less than the quantity y
15. the quantity n plus 4
16. the quantity y minus 4

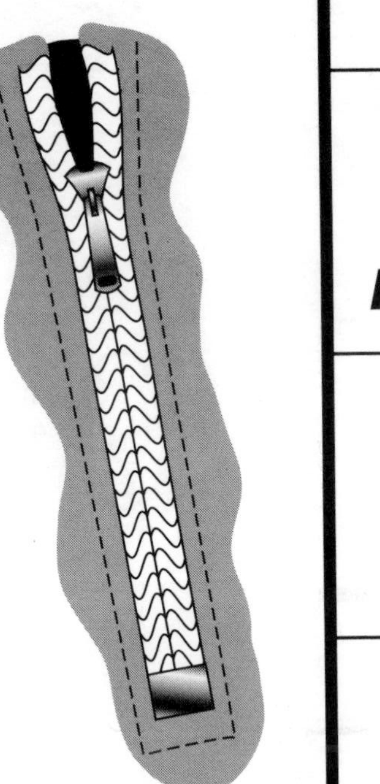

$n/4$	$a + 5$	$y - 4$	$6 + a$
$n + 5$	$n + 12$	$12/a$	$n - 6$
$y - 6$	$n - 3$	$4/n$	$a - 6$
$n - 5$	$4 - n$	$n + 4$	$z + 6$

NCTM Standard: Data Analysis and Probability – formulate questions and analyze data; compute fluently and make reasonable estimates

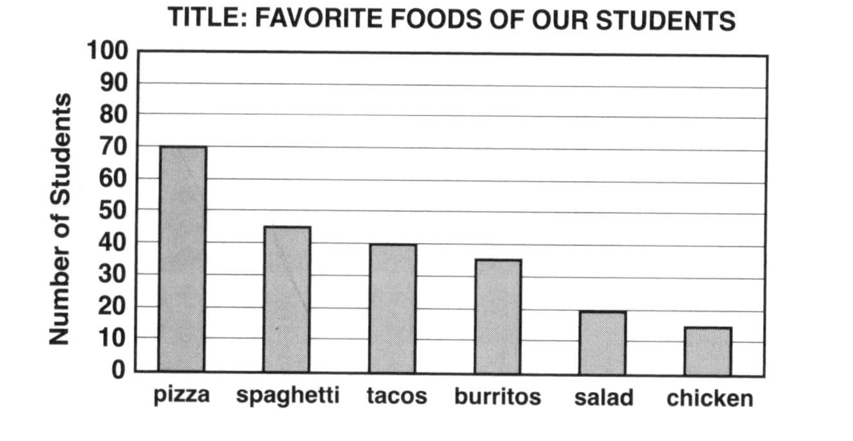

Using the data on the graph, answer the questions below and find the answers in the boxes to the right.

1. What was the least favorite food of the school?
2. What was the favorite food?
3. How many students liked fried chicken?
4. How many more students liked pizza than spaghetti?
5. How many students were in this study?
6. How many students liked burritos and tacos?
7. What was the difference between the fried chicken and the pizza totals?
8. How many students preferred pizza, spaghetti, and tacos?
9. How many preferred burritos, salad, and fried chicken?
10. What percent of all the students liked pizza?
11. What percent of all the students liked fried chicken?
12. What percent of all the students like the top two choices?
13. What was the total number of students minus the total number of students who liked chicken?
14. What was the ratio of pizza students to taco students?
15. What was the ratio of salad students to taco students?

GRIP SOME GRAPHING

75	7%	25
225	70:40	31%
210	chicken	55
155	70	51%
15	20:40	pizza

NCTM Standard: Data Analysis and Probability – analyze data and read various types of graphs

TITLE: How Many Laps Can Students Run in One Week?

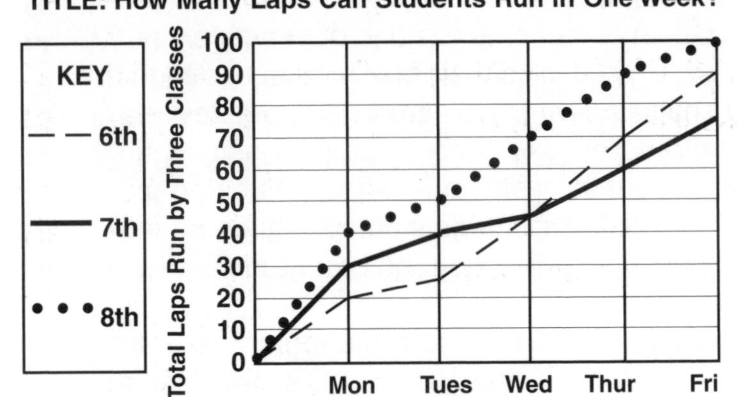

Lap Up Laps

Use the graph to answer the questions below, and find the answers in the boxes to the right.

1. If there were 20 students, how many laps did each seventh grader run on Monday?
2. Who ran the most laps in the five days?
3. Each class had 20 students. How many laps did each eighth grader run on Monday?
4. On Friday, how many laps did each eighth grader run?
5. On what day did the sixth and seventh graders run the same number of laps?
6. On what day were all the grades 10 laps apart?
7. On what day did the sixth grade make the least progress?
8. On Wednesday, what was the difference between the eighth graders and the other two classes?
9. On the last day, how many laps were run by all three classes?
10. What was the total laps run by all classes on Wednesday?
11. On Thursday, what was the difference in the laps of the sixth and seventh graders?
12. What class made a 45-lap increase in two consecutive days?
13. What was the increase in laps from Tuesday to Thursday for the eighth grade?
14. What class made the least progress from Tuesday to Wednesday?
15. How many laps did each seventh grader run on Friday?

160 laps	2 laps	6th grade
5 laps	25 laps	$1\frac{1}{2}$ laps
8th grade	40 laps	Wed.
3.75 laps	Monday	265 laps
Tuesday	7th grade	10 laps

NCTM Standard: Number and Operations – understand the place-value structure of the base ten system

The decimals are written in word form below. Find the matching decimals written in numerical form in the boxes to the right.

1. three and thirty-six ten thousandths
2. three and thirty-six thousandths
3. three and three hundred six ten thousandths
4. thirty-six and thirty-six hundredths
5. three and thirty ten thousandths
6. three and thirteen thousandths
7. thirteen and thirty thousandths
8. thirteen and three thousandths
9. thirteen and three ten thousandths
10. thirty and three hundred six thousandths
11. two and three hundred six ten thousandths
12. two and three hundred six thousandths
13. two and three ten thousandths
14. two and thirty-two thousandths
15. two and thirty-two ten thousandths
16. thirteen and thirty-three thousandths

Earn Some Decimals

Pay to the Order of: $ 13.030

BONUS! 2.0306

13.033	36.36	2.0032	13.003
2.306	13.030	3.036	2.0003
3.0036	3.013	13.0003	30.306
3.0306	2.0306	2.032	3.0030

NCTM Standard: Number and Operations – understand the place-value structure of the base ten system

GET READY TO NAB DECIMALS ON A NUMBER LINE

Determine the decimal that would be at the location of the arrow, and then find the answer in the boxes to the right.

1. 0.255 ↑ 0.257
2. 0.255 ↑ 0.259
3. 0.260 ↑ 0.262
4. 0.260 ↑ 0.268
5. 0.258 ↑ 0.260
6. 0.2550 ↑ 0.2556
7. 0.2550 ↑ 0.2560
8. 0.2550 ↑ 0.2570
9. 0.2550 ↑ 0.2580
10. 0.2550 ↑ 0.2552
11. 0.260 ↑ 0.264
12. 0.260 ↑ 0.300
13. 0.260 ↑ 0.280
14. 0.260 ↑ 0.270
15. 0.2550 ↑ 0.2600

0.265	0.2555	0.261
0.2575	0.256	0.270
0.2565	0.262	0.259
0.257	0.2560	0.2551
0.2553	0.280	0.264

NCTM Standard: Number and Operations – understand numbers and ways of representing numbers

Rack Up Rounding Decimals to the Thousandths

Round the decimals below to the thousandths place, and find the answer in the boxes to the right.

1. 0.40056
2. 0.9009
3. 1.0001
4. 2.9812
5. 6.0115
6. 0.1123
7. 1.0892
8. 2.0433
9. 6.0129
10. 0.4001
11. 1.8999
12. 0.9000
13. 0.1127
14. 2.9999
15. 0.1111

0.401	2.043	3.000
6.013	1.089	0.900
1.000	1.900	2.981
6.012	0.400	0.111
0.112	0.901	0.113

NCTM Standard: Number and Operations – understand numbers and ways of representing numbers

REAP ROUNDING DECIMALS TO THE HUNDREDTHS

Round the following decimals to the hundredths place, and then find the answer in the boxes to the right.

1. 1.568
2. 2.791
3. 0.1222
4. 0.799
5. 3.001
6. 4.008
7. 5.5555
8. 7.0001
9. 0.105
10. 0.309
11. 8.999
12. 0.005
13. 1.011
14. 0.029
15. 3.9569

2.79	1.01	5.56
0.03	1.57	3.96
7.00	0.01	0.31
0.80	9.00	0.12
4.01	0.11	3.00

NCTM Standard: Number and Operations – understand the place-value structure of the base ten system

Slam Dunk Some Decimal Ordering

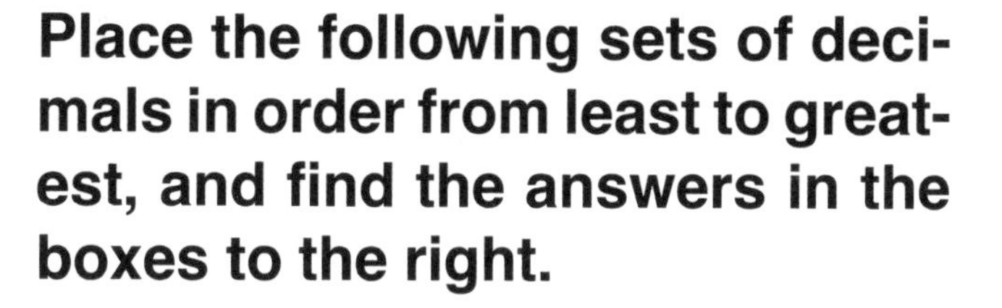

Place the following sets of decimals in order from least to greatest, and find the answers in the boxes to the right.

1. 0.321, 0.322, 0.039
2. 0.321, 0.309, 0.344
3. 0.344, 0.309, 0.039
4. 0.309, 0.039, 0.322
5. 0.344, 0.034, 0.342
6. 0.044, 0.040, 0.401
7. 0.044, 0.049, 0.039
8. 0.040, 0.009, 0.099
9. 0.309, 0.390, 0.004
10. 0.390, 0.300, 0.040
11. 0.309, 0.099, 0.044
12. 0.079, 0.709, 0.907
13. 0.709, 0.799, 0.079
14. 0.709, 0.009, 0.099
15. 0.099, 0.799, 0.009

0.044, 0.099, 0.309	0.009, 0.040, 0.099	0.039, 0.309, 0.322
0.039, 0.321, 0.322	0.009, 0.099, 0.799	0.079, 0.709, 0.799
0.009, 0.099, 0.709	0.034, 0.342, 0.344	0.040, 0.300, 0.390
0.004, 0.309, 0.390	0.039, 0.309, 0.344	0.079, 0.709, 0.907
0.040, 0.044, 0.401	0.039, 0.044, 0.049	0.309, 0.321, 0.344

NCTM Standard: Number and Operations – understand the place-value structure of the base ten system

Swap Some Decimal Values

This is a series of six digits: 1, 2, 3, 4, 7, 9. Put the digits in an order to make a number closest to the following descriptions. Then find the answer in the boxes to the right.

1. closest to 10
2. closest to 12
3. closest to 27
4. closest to 28
5. closest to 13
6. closest to 14
7. closest to 8
8. closest to 3
9. closest to 6
10. closest to 15
11. closest to 16
12. closest to 20
13. closest to 21
14. closest to 35
15. closest to 37

34.9721	12.3479	7.94321
4.97321	12.9743	21.3479
27.1349	19.7432	13.9742
37.1249	14.9732	27.9431
9.74321	2.97431	17.2349

NCTM Standard: Number and Operations – understand the place-value structure of the base ten system

Sweep Up Decimals

Determine the decimal numeral represented by the dots in each place below, and find the matching number in the boxes to the right.

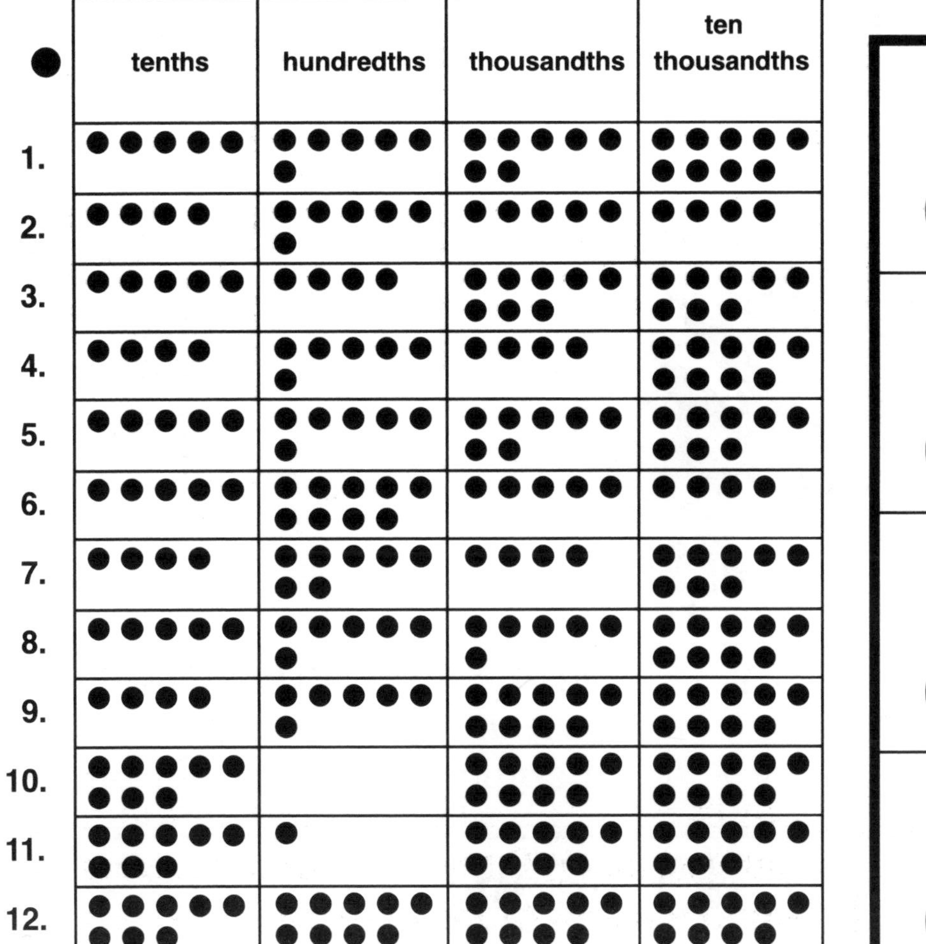

0.4699	0.5679	0.5954
0.5488	0.4748	0.8198
0.8099	0.4649	0.8999
0.5669	0.4654	0.5678

NCTM Standard: Number and Operations – understand numbers and ways of representing numbers

Sweop Up Rounding Decimals

Round the following numbers to the tenths place. Then find the answers in the boxes to the right.

1. 1.23
2. 0.39
3. 0.658
4. 0.798
5. 0.3421
6. 0.21
7. 1.79
8. 2.71
9. 0.8944
10. 0.95
11. 4.7211
12. 0.015
13. 0.0982
14. 1.999
15. 3.0127

0.3	1.2	0.1
2.7	0.0	0.4
0.7	3.0	4.7
1.0	2.0	0.9
0.2	0.8	1.8

NCTM Standard: Number and Operations – understand the place-value structure of the base ten system

TAG SOME ORDERED DECIMALS

0.24, 0.29, 0.42

0.04, 0.05, 0.40

Place the following sets of decimals in the order from least to greatest, and find the answers in the boxes to the right.

1. 0.03, 0.33, 0.3
2. 0.33, 0.35, 0.03
3. 0.33, 0.3, 0.32
4. 0.34, 0.53, 0.03
5. 0.35, 0.25, 0.33
6. 0.34, 0.33, 0.29
7. 0.34, 0.43, 0.42
8. 0.42, 0.24, 0.29
9. 0.42, 0.39, 0.4
10. 0.4, 0.39, 0.04
11. 0.03, 0.30, 0.29
12. 0.04, 0.40, 0.05
13. 0.05, 0.38, 0.39
14. 0.05, 0.50, 0.29
15. 0.39, 0.92, 0.90

0.25, 0.33, 0.35	**0.04, 0.05, 0.40**	**0.04, 0.39, 0.4**
0.05, 0.29, 0.50	**0.24, 0.29, 0.42**	**0.03, 0.34, 0.53**
0.03, 0.3, 0.33	**0.39, 0.90, 0.92**	**0.34, 0.42, 0.43**
0.03, 0.29, 0.30	**0.3, 0.32, 0.33**	**0.05, 0.38, 0.39**
0.29, 0.33, 0.34	**0.39, 0.4, 0.42**	**0.03, 0.33, 0.35**

NCTM Standard: Number and Operations – compute fluently; make reasonable estimates; understand the base ten system

Ambush Some Decimal Round-ups

Round all the decimals below to the tenths place, and then estimate the answers. Find the correct answers in the boxes to the right.

1. 0.567 x 0.432 =
2. 0.55 x 0.67 =
3. 0.312 x 0.521 =
4. 0.34 x 0.56 =
5. 0.567 x 0.89 =
6. 0.421 x 0.544 =
7. 0.598 x 0.522 =
8. 0.943 x 0.45 =
9. 0.192 x 0.542 =
10. 0.24 x 0.567 =
11. 0.221 x 0.841 =
12. 0.78 x 0.93 =
13. 0.298 x 0.943 =
14. 0.798 x 0.817 =
15. 0.902 x 0.724 =
16. 0.54 x 0.789 =

0.64	0.24	0.63	0.10
0.30	0.16	0.15	0.40
0.42	0.45	0.27	0.54
0.20	0.72	0.18	0.12

NCTM Standard: Number and Operations – compute fluently; **Algebra** – use symbolic algebra to represent problems

Dive for Decimal Quotient Unknowns

Solve the problems below by finding the unknown decimal quotients in each. Find the correct answers in the boxes to the right.

1. $420 \div 0.7 = n$
2. $640 \div 0.08 = m$
3. $540 \div 0.6 = t$
4. $320 \div 0.8 = y$
5. $200 \div 0.2 = a$
6. $810 \div 0.3 = n$
7. $400 \div 0.8 = m$
8. $250 \div 0.05 = t$
9. $240 \div 0.12 = y$
10. $300 \div 0.05 = a$
11. $180 \div 0.6 = n$
12. $160 \div 0.04 = m$
13. $500 \div 0.2 = t$
14. $600 \div 0.2 = y$
15. $700 \div 0.2 = a$

300	900	4,000
2,700	2,500	1,000
2,000	500	400
8,000	3,500	6,000
3,000	5,000	600

EXTRACT SOME DECIMAL DIVISION ESTIMATES

Estimate the division problems below, and find the matching range of the quotient to each in the boxes to the right.

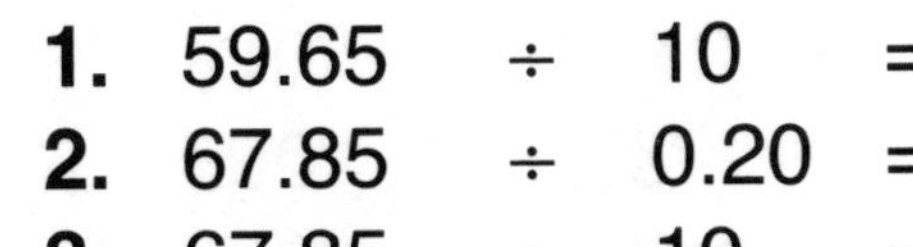

1. 59.65 ÷ 10 =
2. 67.85 ÷ 0.20 =
3. 67.85 ÷ 10 =
4. 0.5789 ÷ 0.20 =
5. 0.6785 ÷ 10 =
6. 0.5965 ÷ 20 =
7. 5.789 ÷ 10 =
8. 6.785 ÷ 20 =
9. 5,789 ÷ 10 =
10. 69.65 ÷ 0.10 =
11. 5.789 ÷ 0.20 =
12. 57.89 ÷ 50 =
13. 578.9 ÷ 50 =
14. 6.785 ÷ 0.50 =
15. 5,965 ÷ 50 =

between 20 & 30	between 5 & 6	between 2 & 3
between 300 & 400	between 11 & 12	between 600 & 700
between 13 & 14	between 6 & 7	between 0.3 & 0.4
between 0.06 & 0.07	between 0.5 & 0.6	between 100 & 200
between 500 & 600	between 1 & 2	between 0.02 & 0.03

NCTM Standard: Number and Operations – compute fluently and make reasonable estimates

Groove With Decimal Multiples

Try to mentally calculate the following problems, and then find the answers in the boxes to the right.

1. 0.5 x 500 =
2. 0.2 x 300 =
3. 0.3 x 600 =
4. 0.3 x 220 =
5. 0.6 x 200 =
6. 0.7 x 300 =
7. 0.8 x 400 =
8. 0.9 x 800 =
9. 0.3 x 300 =
10. 0.4 x 400 =
11. 0.4 x 500 =
12. 0.5 x 300 =
13. 0.6 x 400 =
14. 0.7 x 400 =
15. 0.9 x 300 =

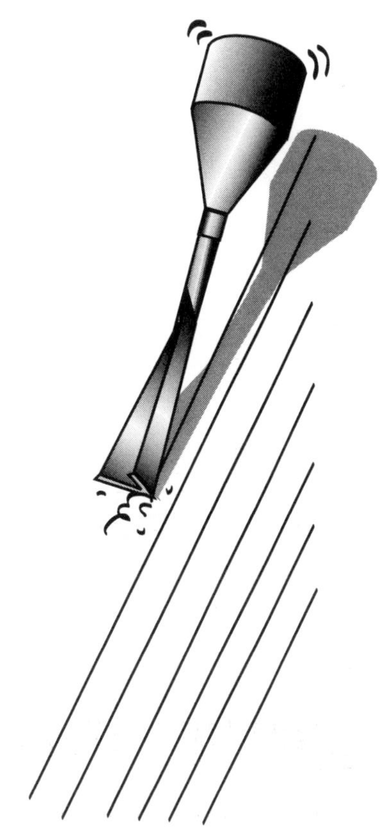

280	210	60
240	150	160
66	250	720
320	200	120
180	90	270

NCTM Standard: Number and Operations – compute fluently and make reasonable estimates

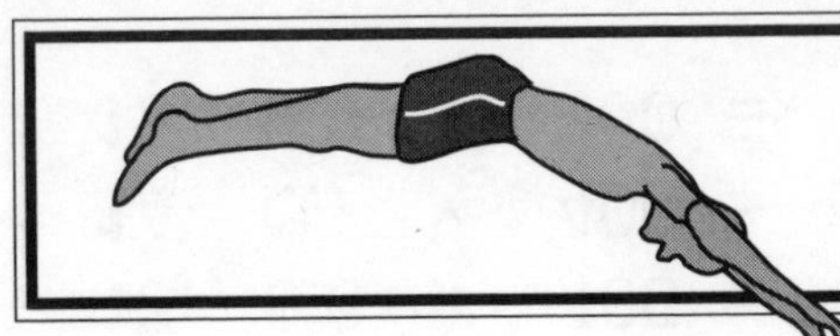

Dive Into Challenging Division

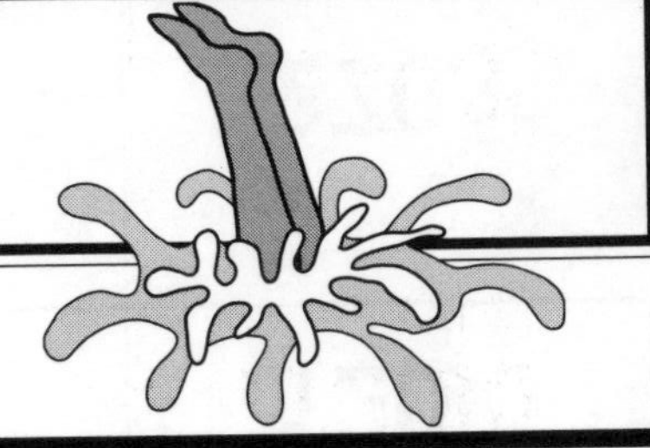

<u>Estimate</u> the following problems by rounding the dividend to a compatible number. Find the answer in the boxes to the right.

1. 27,302 ÷ 90 =
2. 29,100 ÷ 70 =
3. 75,200 ÷ 75 =
4. 73,102 ÷ 80 =
5. 87,900 ÷ 110 =
6. 62,899 ÷ 700 =
7. 49,798 ÷ 10 =
8. 36,101 ÷ 1,200 =
9. 24,897 ÷ 50 =
10. 29,099 ÷ 10 =
11. 72,123 ÷ 900 =
12. 66,213 ÷ 1,000 =
13. 31,978 ÷ 50 =
14. 41,870 ÷ 60 =
15. 17,999 ÷ 90 =
16. 18,101 ÷ 900 =

400	80	200	66
90	900	30	500
1,000	600	20	800
5,000	700	3,000	300

NCTM Standard: Number and Operations – understand proportions and represent quantitative relationships

Pounce on Proportions

Below are a number of proportions. Solve these by cross-multiplying, and then find the correct answer for each in the boxes on the right.

1. $\frac{1}{2} = \frac{n}{6}$
2. $\frac{5}{8} = \frac{n}{15}$
3. $\frac{5}{7} = \frac{20}{n}$
4. $\frac{n}{4} = \frac{16}{20}$
5. $\frac{10}{n} = \frac{15}{45}$
6. $\frac{5}{n} = \frac{12}{5}$
7. $\frac{8}{9} = \frac{12}{n}$
8. $\frac{3}{n} = \frac{24}{4}$
9. $\frac{n}{9} = \frac{15}{27}$
10. $\frac{4}{n} = \frac{16}{8}$
11. $\frac{n}{5} = \frac{30}{6}$
12. $\frac{6}{n} = \frac{30}{8}$
13. $\frac{5}{n} = \frac{25}{20}$
14. $\frac{n}{6} = \frac{28}{7}$
15. $\frac{8}{12} = \frac{n}{15}$

$n = 28$	$n = 0.5$	$n = 25$
$n = 5$	$n = 24$	$n = 13.5$
$n = 1.6$	$n = 9.375$	$n = 10$
$n = 2.08\overline{3}$	$n = 4$	$n = 30$
$n = 3.2$	$n = 2$	$n = 3$

NCTM Standard: Number and Operations – understand ways of representing numbers; make reasonable estimates

Search for a Square Root

Find the square root of each number below. The answers have been rounded and are in the boxes to the right.

1. 144
2. 140
3. 35
4. 68
5. 64
6. 28
7. 9
8. 8
9. 26
10. 65
11. 119
12. 25
13. 148
14. 121
15. 12

3.46	5.10	11
5	8.2	12
8.06	11.8	8
10.9	3	2.8
5.3	5.9	12.17

NCTM Standard: Number and Operations – make reasonable estimates

Strike Out Square Roots

If the square root of 25 is 5 and the square root of 36 is 6, then the square root of 26 is somewhere between 5 and 6. Estimate which square root to the right would be at the place of the arrow for each item below.

1. 28 ↑ 30
2. 36 ↑ 40
3. 40 ↑ 50
4. 50 ↑ 60
5. 60 ↑ 64
6. 70 ↑ 72
7. 75 ↑ 77
8. 34 ↑ 36
9. 48 ↑ 50
10. 60 ↑ 68
11. 78 ↑ 84
12. 98 ↑ 102
13. 80 ↑ 90
14. 10 ↑ 20
15. 12 ↑ 14

8	7.874	3.873
8.426	6.164	3.6
5.916	10	6.7
5.385	7	9.22
8.718	7.416	9

NCTM Standard: Number and Operations – compute fluently and make reasonable estimates; use mental computation to estimate fractions

Bring in a Flood of Quotients

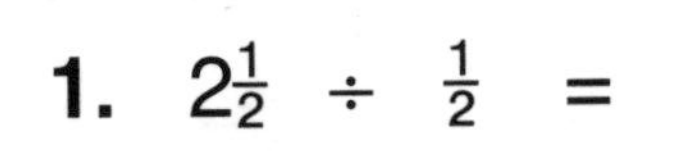

See if you can solve the following fraction problems by "visualizing" the dividend. Then find the answer in the boxes to the right.

1. $2\frac{1}{2} \div \frac{1}{2} =$
2. $2\frac{1}{2} \div \frac{1}{4} =$
3. $6\frac{1}{8} \div \frac{1}{8} =$
4. $2\frac{3}{4} \div \frac{1}{4} =$
5. $2\frac{1}{4} \div \frac{3}{4} =$
6. $3\frac{1}{2} \div \frac{1}{4} =$
7. $6\frac{7}{8} \div \frac{1}{8} =$
8. $4\frac{1}{2} \div \frac{1}{2} =$
9. $6\frac{1}{2} \div \frac{1}{4} =$
10. $3\frac{1}{2} \div \frac{1}{2} =$
11. $4\frac{1}{2} \div \frac{1}{4} =$
12. $1\frac{1}{2} \div \frac{1}{4} =$
13. $5\frac{1}{4} \div \frac{1}{8} =$
14. $6\frac{1}{2} \div \frac{1}{8} =$
15. $1\frac{1}{2} \div \frac{3}{4} =$
16. $2\frac{7}{8} \div \frac{1}{8} =$

11	18	6	49
42	23	9	55
2	10	14	52
5	26	7	3

NCTM Standard: Number and Operations – compute fluently and make reasonable estimates; use mental computation to estimate fractions

CONQUER MULTIPLYING MIXED NUMBERS

Multiply the mixed numbers times the whole numbers below, and find the answers in the boxes to the right.

1. $2\frac{1}{2} \times 6 =$		**9.** $1\frac{1}{4} \times 9 =$	
2. $1\frac{1}{2} \times 2 =$		**10.** $3\frac{1}{3} \times 3 =$	
3. $3\frac{1}{2} \times 3 =$		**11.** $1\frac{1}{2} \times 9 =$	
4. $2\frac{1}{4} \times 4 =$		**12.** $2\frac{1}{3} \times 6 =$	
5. $2\frac{1}{4} \times 8 =$		**13.** $1\frac{1}{3} \times 6 =$	
6. $1\frac{1}{2} \times 3 =$		**14.** $1\frac{1}{5} \times 10 =$	
7. $1\frac{1}{2} \times 5 =$		**15.** $2\frac{1}{5} \times 10 =$	
8. $2\frac{1}{8} \times 8 =$		**16.** $3\frac{1}{2} \times 1 =$	

$11\frac{1}{4}$	10	9	18
$10\frac{1}{2}$	22	3	8
$4\frac{1}{2}$	15	$3\frac{1}{2}$	17
$13\frac{1}{2}$	12	$7\frac{1}{2}$	14

NCTM Standard: Number and Operations – compute fluently; select appropriate methods for fraction computation

Finding Fractional Parts of Whole Numbers

Find the fractional part of each whole number in the problems below, and find the answer in the boxes to the right.

1. $\frac{1}{2}$ of 12 =

2. $\frac{1}{4}$ of 16 =

3. $\frac{1}{5}$ of 25 =

4. $\frac{1}{2}$ of 60 =

5. $\frac{1}{5}$ of 50 =

6. $\frac{1}{3}$ of 36 =

7. $\frac{1}{2}$ of 48 =

8. $\frac{1}{3}$ of 150 =

9. $\frac{1}{4}$ of 44 =

10. $\frac{1}{4}$ of 400 =

11. $\frac{1}{5}$ of 100 =

12. $\frac{1}{2}$ of 90 =

13. $\frac{1}{4}$ of 160 =

14. $\frac{1}{5}$ of 350 =

15. $\frac{1}{3}$ of 81 =

16. $\frac{1}{3}$ of 180 =

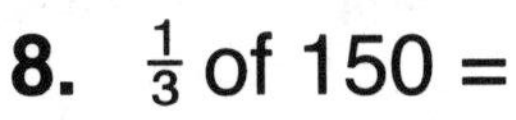

100	**24**	**60**	**20**
5	**6**	**45**	**10**
30	**27**	**4**	**11**
40	**50**	**70**	**12**

NCTM Standard: Number and Operations – understand ways of representing numbers

The lines below represent some fractions. In the boxes to the right, find the fraction that would be where the arrow is located.

Grasp a Fractional Location

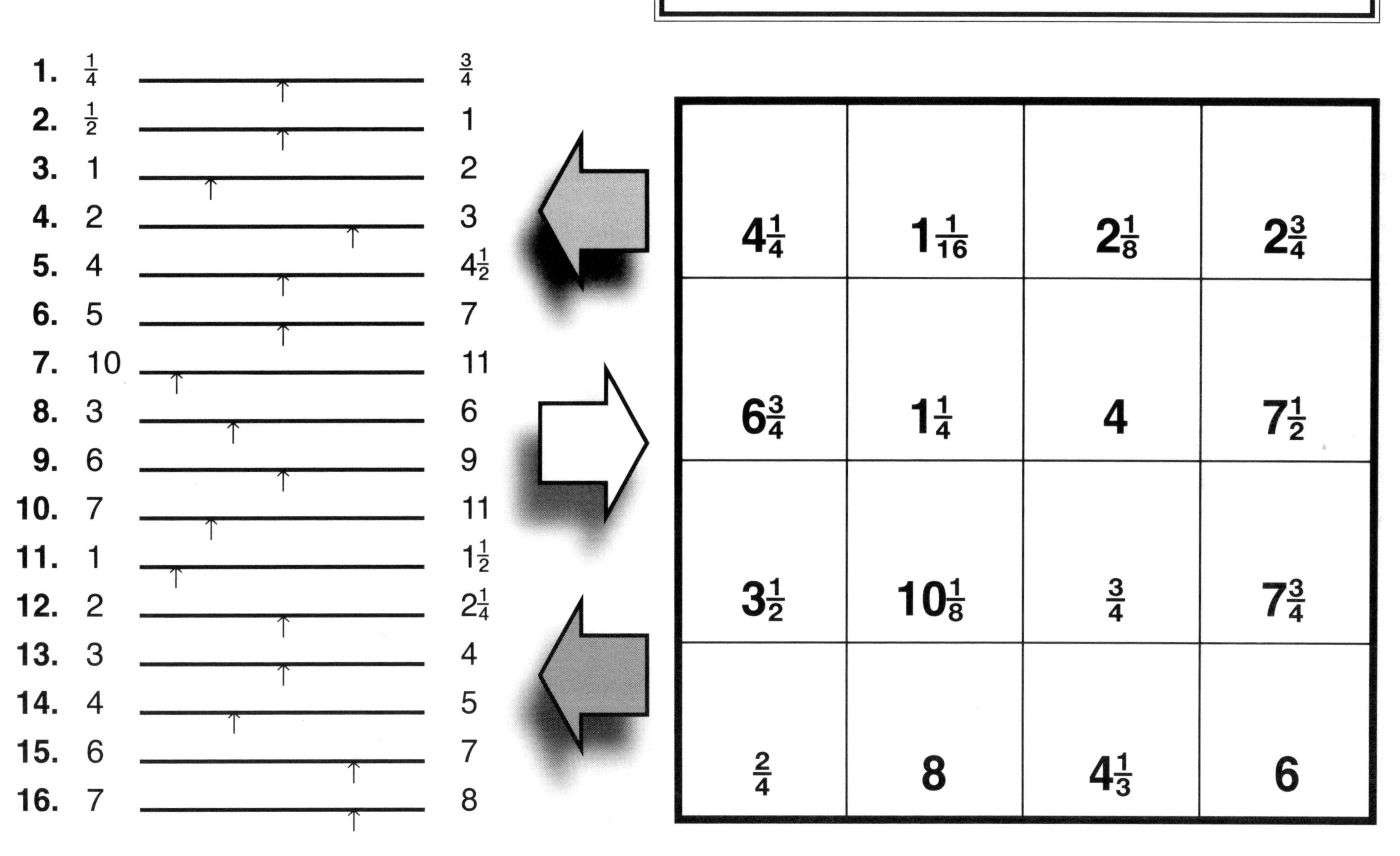

1. $\frac{1}{4}$ — $\frac{3}{4}$
2. $\frac{1}{2}$ — 1
3. 1 — 2
4. 2 — 3
5. 4 — $4\frac{1}{2}$
6. 5 — 7
7. 10 — 11
8. 3 — 6
9. 6 — 9
10. 7 — 11
11. 1 — $1\frac{1}{2}$
12. 2 — $2\frac{1}{4}$
13. 3 — 4
14. 4 — 5
15. 6 — 7
16. 7 — 8

$4\frac{1}{4}$	$1\frac{1}{16}$	$2\frac{1}{8}$	$2\frac{3}{4}$
$6\frac{3}{4}$	$1\frac{1}{4}$	4	$7\frac{1}{2}$
$3\frac{1}{2}$	$10\frac{1}{8}$	$\frac{3}{4}$	$7\frac{3}{4}$
$\frac{2}{4}$	8	$4\frac{1}{3}$	6

NCTM Standard: Number and Operations – understand ways of representing numbers

The lines below represent some fractions. In the boxes to the right, find the fraction that would be where the arrow is located.

LOCK ONTO A FRACTION

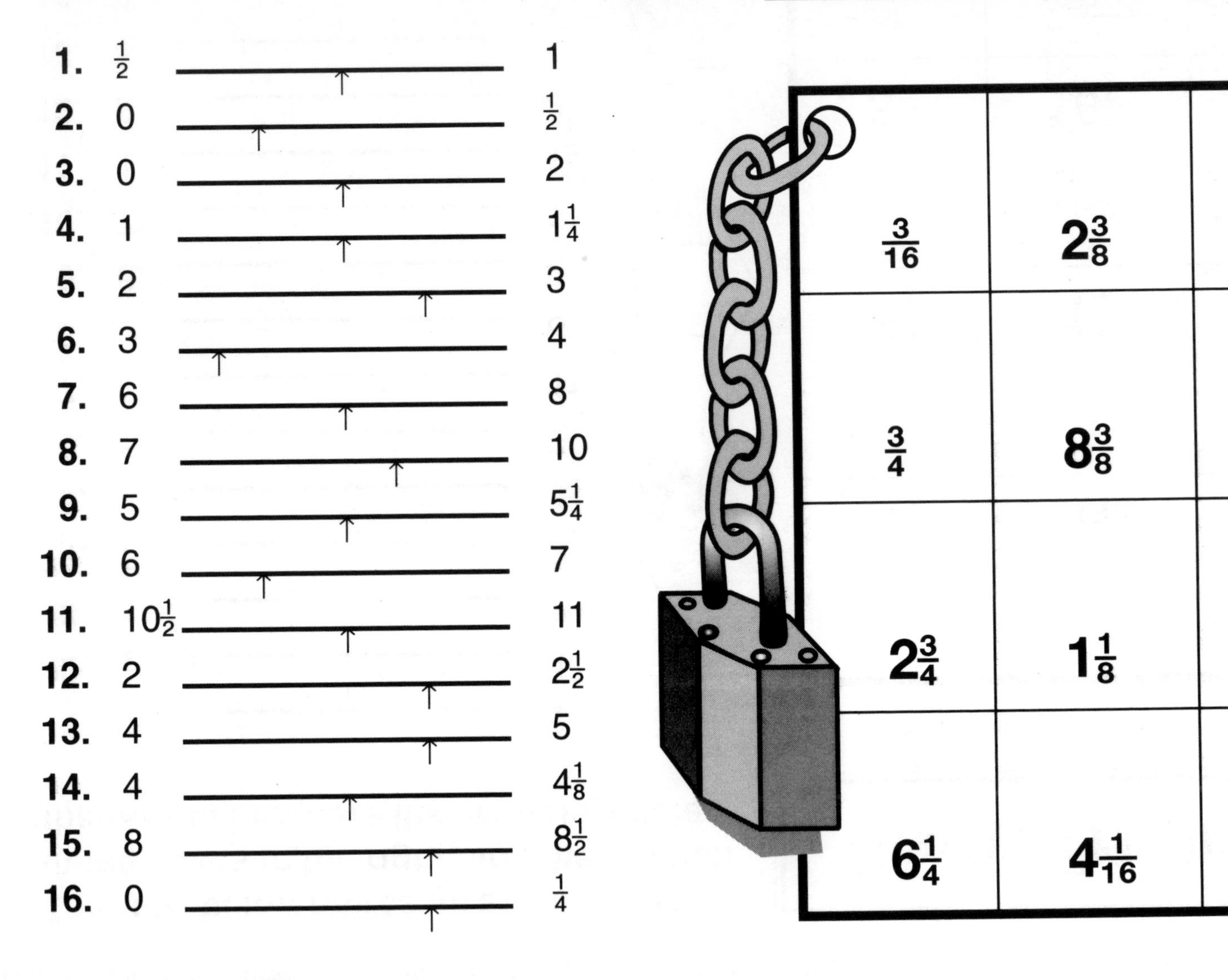

1. $\frac{1}{2}$ ——— 1
2. 0 ——— $\frac{1}{2}$
3. 0 ——— 2
4. 1 ——— $1\frac{1}{4}$
5. 2 ——— 3
6. 3 ——— 4
7. 6 ——— 8
8. 7 ——— 10
9. 5 ——— $5\frac{1}{4}$
10. 6 ——— 7
11. $10\frac{1}{2}$ ——— 11
12. 2 ——— $2\frac{1}{2}$
13. 4 ——— 5
14. 4 ——— $4\frac{1}{8}$
15. 8 ——— $8\frac{1}{2}$
16. 0 ——— $\frac{1}{4}$

$\frac{3}{16}$	$2\frac{3}{8}$	7	$\frac{1}{8}$
$\frac{3}{4}$	$8\frac{3}{8}$	$5\frac{1}{8}$	$10\frac{3}{4}$
$2\frac{3}{4}$	$1\frac{1}{8}$	$4\frac{3}{4}$	9
$6\frac{1}{4}$	$4\frac{1}{16}$	$3\frac{1}{8}$	1

NCTM Standard: Number and Operations – compute fluently and use mental calculation to compute fractions

Win a Product

Multiply the fractions and whole numbers in the problems below. Then find the answers in the boxes to the right.

1. $\frac{1}{2}$ x 70 =
2. $\frac{1}{2}$ x 90 =
3. $\frac{3}{4}$ x 80 =
4. $\frac{3}{4}$ x 200 =
5. $\frac{1}{2}$ x 50 =
6. $\frac{1}{2}$ x 24 =
7. $\frac{3}{4}$ x 24 =
8. $\frac{3}{4}$ x 160 =
9. $\frac{1}{2}$ x 150 =
10. $\frac{1}{5}$ x 150 =
11. $\frac{1}{5}$ x 20 =
12. $\frac{1}{5}$ x 30 =
13. $\frac{1}{4}$ x 20 =
14. $\frac{1}{4}$ x 80 =
15. $\frac{1}{5}$ x 50 =

120	10	45
20	12	5
4	35	18
6	25	30
150	75	60

NCTM Standard: Number and Operations – understand ways of representing numbers; work flexibly with fractions and decimals

Finding Fraction-Decimal Equivalents

Find the fraction equivalents of the following decimals in the boxes to the right.

1. 0.25
2. 0.5
3. 0.4
4. 0.2
5. 0.02
6. 0.05
7. 0.8
8. 0.025
9. 0.040
10. 0.08
11. 0.6
12. 0.020
13. 0.06
14. 0.008
15. 0.006

$\frac{2}{10}$	$\frac{40}{1000}$	$\frac{20}{1000}$
$\frac{5}{100}$	$\frac{6}{10}$	$\frac{5}{10}$
$\frac{4}{10}$	$\frac{8}{10}$	$\frac{8}{1000}$
$\frac{6}{100}$	$\frac{25}{100}$	$\frac{6}{1000}$
$\frac{25}{1000}$	$\frac{2}{100}$	$\frac{8}{100}$

NCTM Standard: Number and Operations – understand ways of representing numbers; work flexibly with fractions, decimals, and percents

GRAB ON TO FRACTION-DECIMAL-PERCENT EQUIVALENTS

In each item below are two equivalent fractions, decimals, or percents. Find the third matching equivalent for each item in the boxes to the right.

1. 50% 0.50 ______
2. $\frac{3}{4}$ 75% ______
3. 45% 0.45 ______
4. 0.2 $\frac{1}{5}$ ______
5. 80% $\frac{4}{5}$ ______
6. 0.40 40% ______
7. 60% $\frac{3}{5}$ ______
8. $\frac{2}{5}$ 0.4 ______
9. $\frac{5}{8}$ 0.625 ______
10. 87.5% 0.875 ______
11. 60% 0.6 ______
12. 0.35 35% ______
13. $\frac{1}{4}$ 0.25 ______
14. 12.5% 0.125 ______
15. 70% 0.7 ______
16. 0.9 $\frac{9}{10}$ ______

$\frac{7}{8}$	**40%**	**0.8**	$\frac{9}{20}$
20%	$\frac{3}{5}$	**25%**	$\frac{1}{2}$
$\frac{7}{20}$	$\frac{1}{8}$	$\frac{2}{5}$	$\frac{7}{10}$
0.75	**62.5%**	**90%**	**0.6**

NCTM Standard: Geometry – understand relationships among two-dimensional objects, using defining properties such as perimeter, area, surface area, and volume

Buffalo Some Triangular Perimeters

Determine the perimeter of each triangle in the boxes to the right. Match the perimeters below with the correct triangles to the right.

1. 32 inches
2. 12.8 inches
3. 27.4 inches
4. 29.3 inches
5. 23.4 inches
6. 49.5 inches
7. 43 inches
8. 18.8 inches
9. 15.7 inches
10. 18.2 inches
11. 17.9 inches
12. 15.2 inches
13. 44.5 inches
14. 24 inches
15. 20.9 inches

9″, 7″, 11.4″	7″, 7.2″, 4″	10″, 10″, 12″
8″, 8″, 8″	9″, 9.3″, 5.1″	14″, 15″, 20.5″
15″, 19″, 10.5″	3″, 6″, 6.7″	7.3″, 7.6″, 3″
10″, 18″, 15″	12″, 12.3″, 5″	3.2″, 6″, 3.6″
8″, 4″, 8.9″	3.1″, 7″, 5.1″	5″, 5.6″, 8.2″

NCTM Standard: Geometry – understand relationships among two-dimensional objects; be able to calculate area, surface area, and volume

DIVE INTO TRIANGULAR AREAS

Find the area of each triangle to the right. Match the areas below with the correct triangles in the boxes to the right.

1. 20 square inches
2. 36 square inches
3. $10\frac{1}{2}$ square inches
4. 45 square inches
5. 225 square inches
6. 6 square inches
7. 60 square inches
8. $27\frac{1}{2}$ square inches
9. 12 square inches
10. 25 square inches
11. 30 square inches
12. 75 square inches
13. 14 square inches
14. 375 square inches
15. 450 square inches

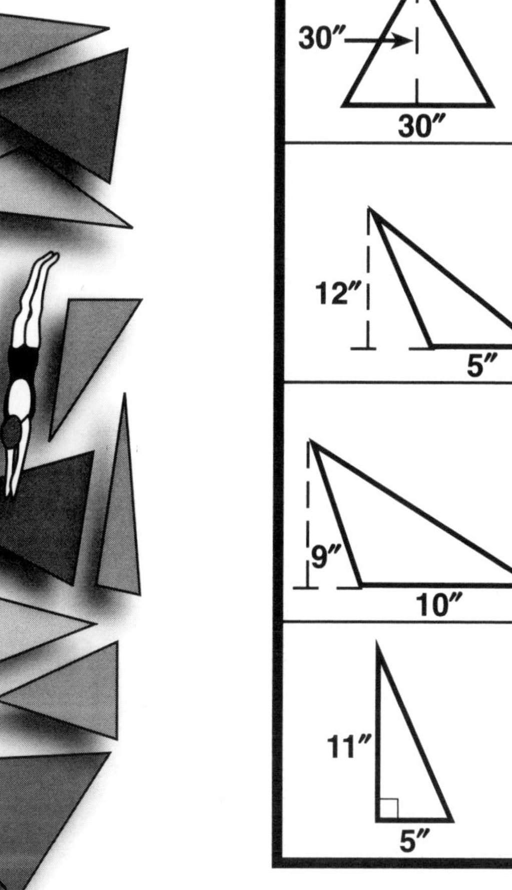

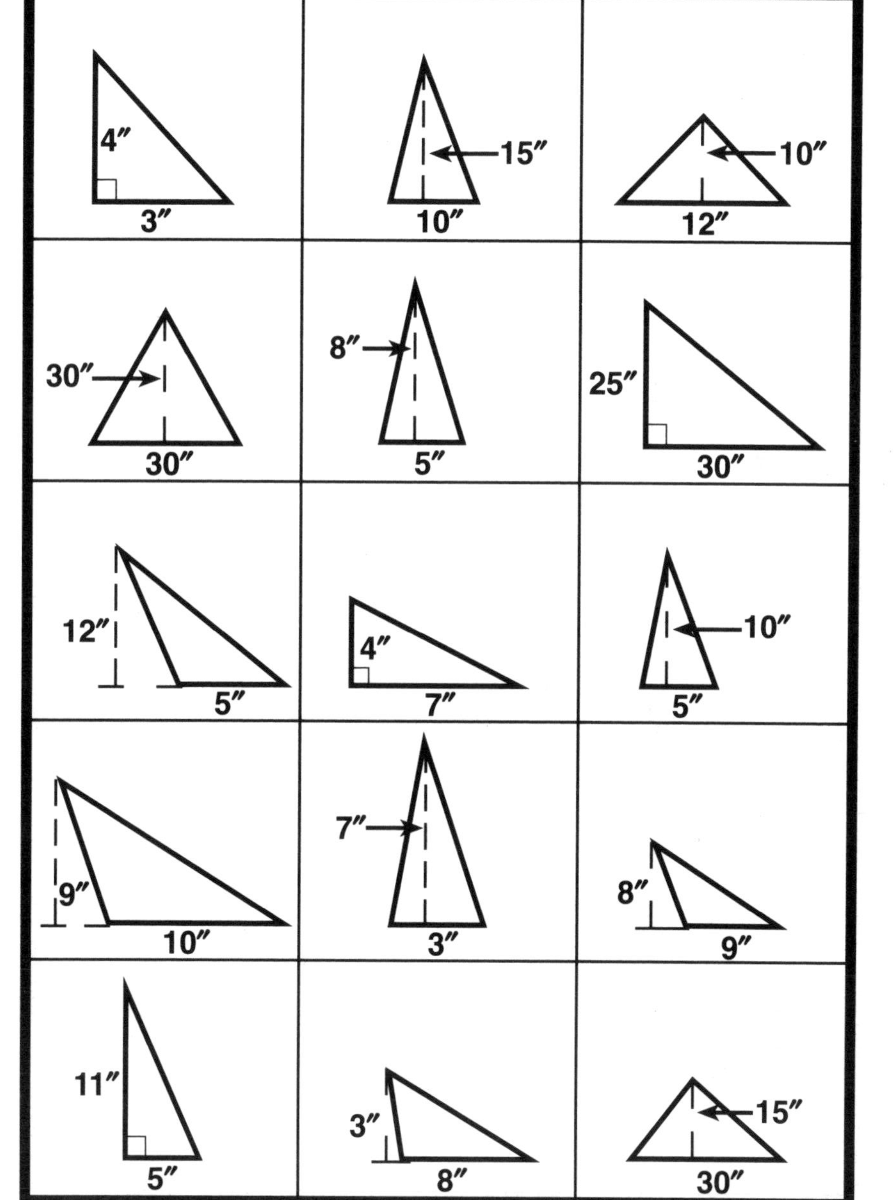

NCTM Standard: Geometry – identify three-dimensional geometric shapes

Fetch Figures in Space

Match the name of each geometric figure below with the correct figure in the boxes to the right.

1. hexagonal prism
2. square pyramid
3. triangular prism
4. octagonal prism
5. oblique cylinder
6. rectangular prism
7. cylinder
8. cube
9. hexagonal pyramid
10. cone
11. octagonal pyramid
12. triangular pyramid

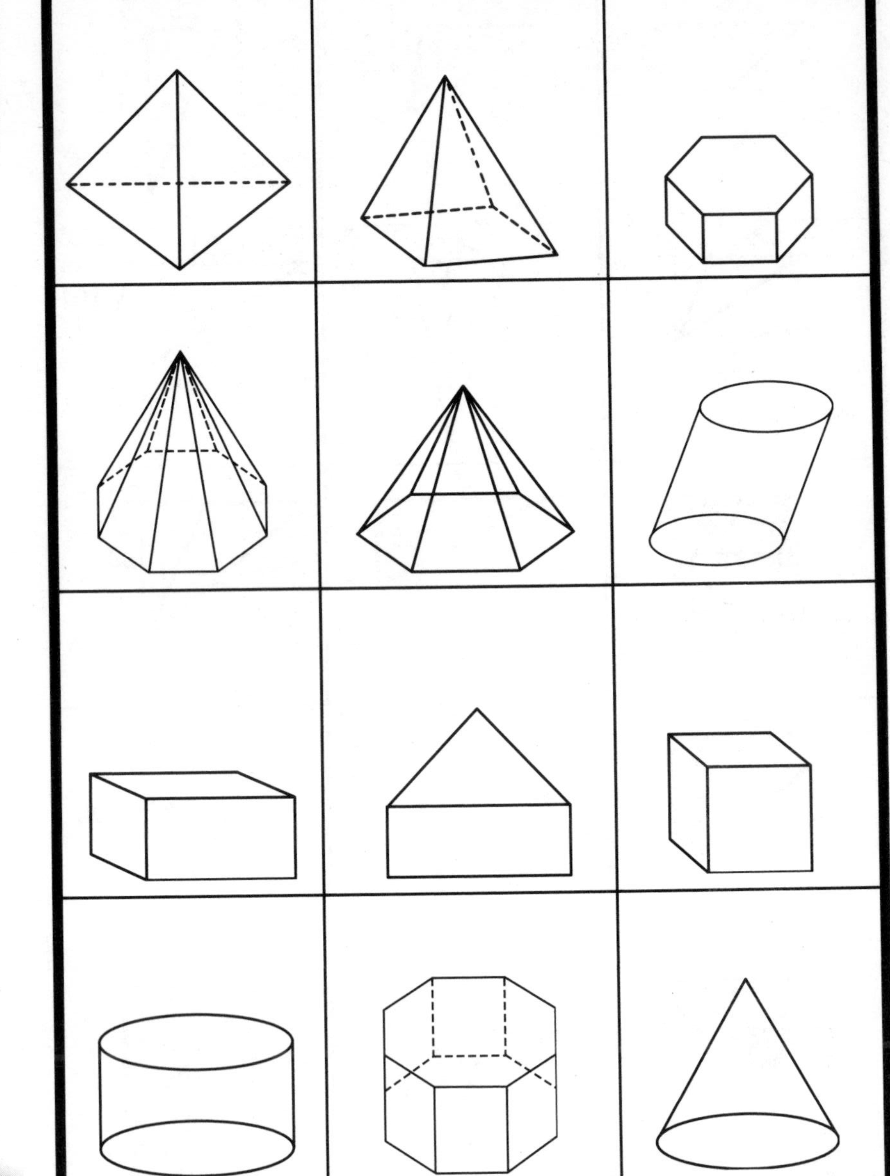

NCTM Standard: Geometry – specify locations using coordinate geometry

Grab a Coordinate

Find the coordinates in the boxes to the right that match each numbered point in the coordinate graph below.

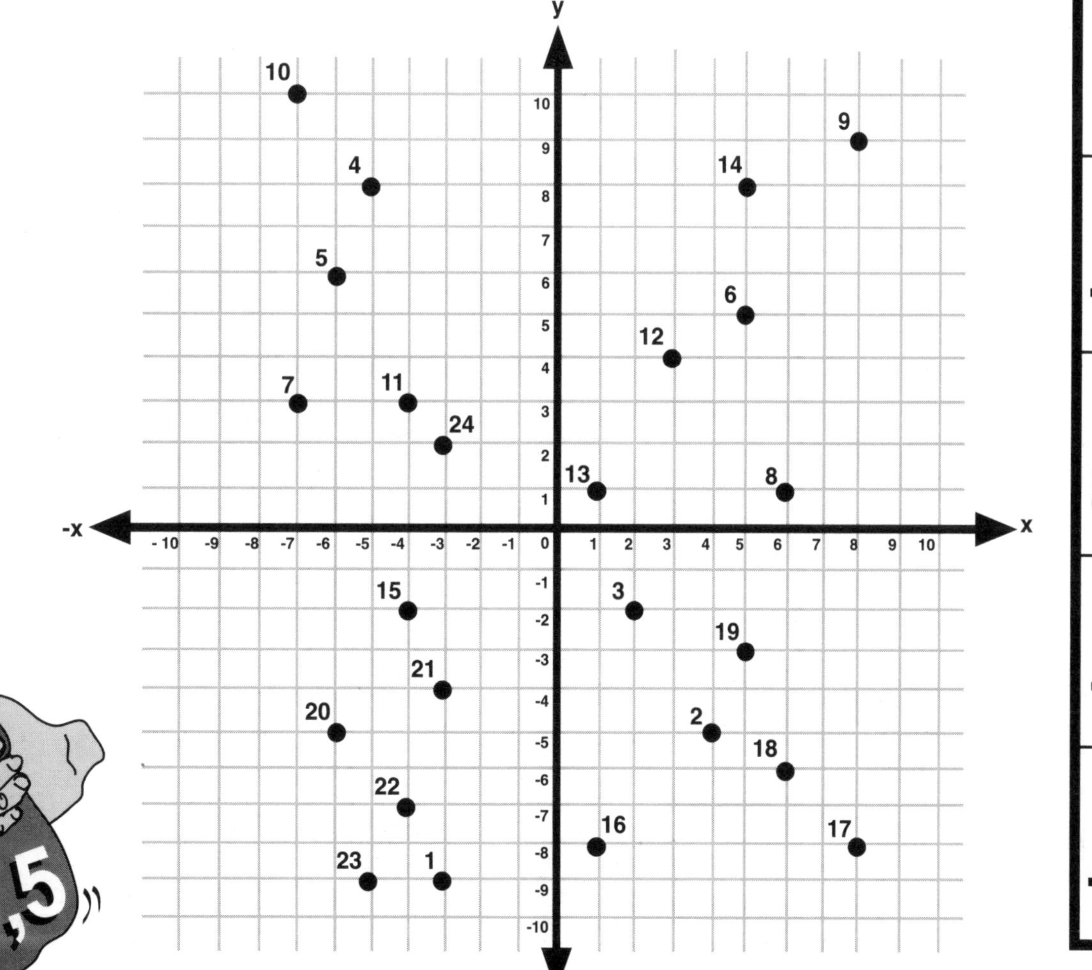

3,4	5,-3	2,-2	5,8
1,-8	4,-5	-4,-7	5,5
-7,3	6,-6	-4,3	-3,-9
8,-8	1,1	-6,-5	-4,-2
-5,8	-3,2	-7,10	-5,-9
-3,-4	8,9	-6,6	6,1

NCTM Standard: Geometry – analyze properties of two-dimensional shapes or objects

Lasso Lines and Points

Read the definitions below, and find the corresponding answer in the boxes to the right.

The name:

1. of an exact location
2. of a piece of a line with 2 endpoints
3. of two lines that are an exact distance apart and that never meet
4. of two lines that are in different planes and are neither parallel nor intersecting
5. of two lines that meet and form right angles
6. of a line that bends and can form an opened or closed figure
7. of a line that goes in one direction without stopping and has one endpoint
8. of two rays that have a common endpoint
9. of an angle that measures 180°
10. of two angles that add up to 180°
11. of two angles that together add up to 90°
12. of a ray that separates an angle into two congruent angles
13. of the tool used to measure angles
14. of the point of an angle
15. of an angle that is less than 90°
16. of an angle that is more than 90°

angle	pro-tractor	acute angle	parallel lines
straight angle	point	comple-mentary angles	line segment
perpen-dicular lines	curve	angle bisector	obtuse angle
ray	skew lines	vertex	supple-mentary angles

NCTM Standard: Geometry – analyze properties of two-dimensional geometric shapes; understand relationships among areas of shapes

LATCH ON TO TWO-DIMENSIONAL AREAS

Find the areas of each of the shapes to the right. Then match the answers below to the shapes in the boxes to the right.

1. 72 square inches
2. 78.5 square inches
3. 17.5 square inches
4. 105 square inches
5. 30 square inches
6. 66 square inches
7. 20 square inches
8. 40 square inches
9. 300 square inches
10. 28 square inches
11. 113.04 square inches
12. 54 square inches
13. 60 square inches
14. 16 square inches
15. 21 square inches
16. 33 square inches

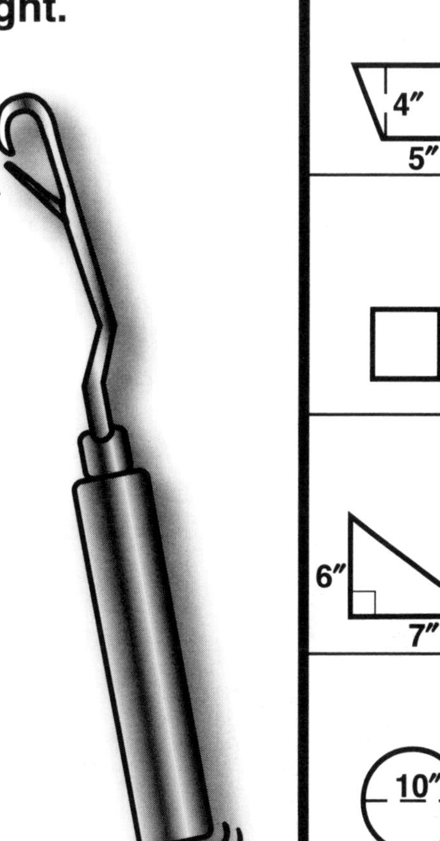

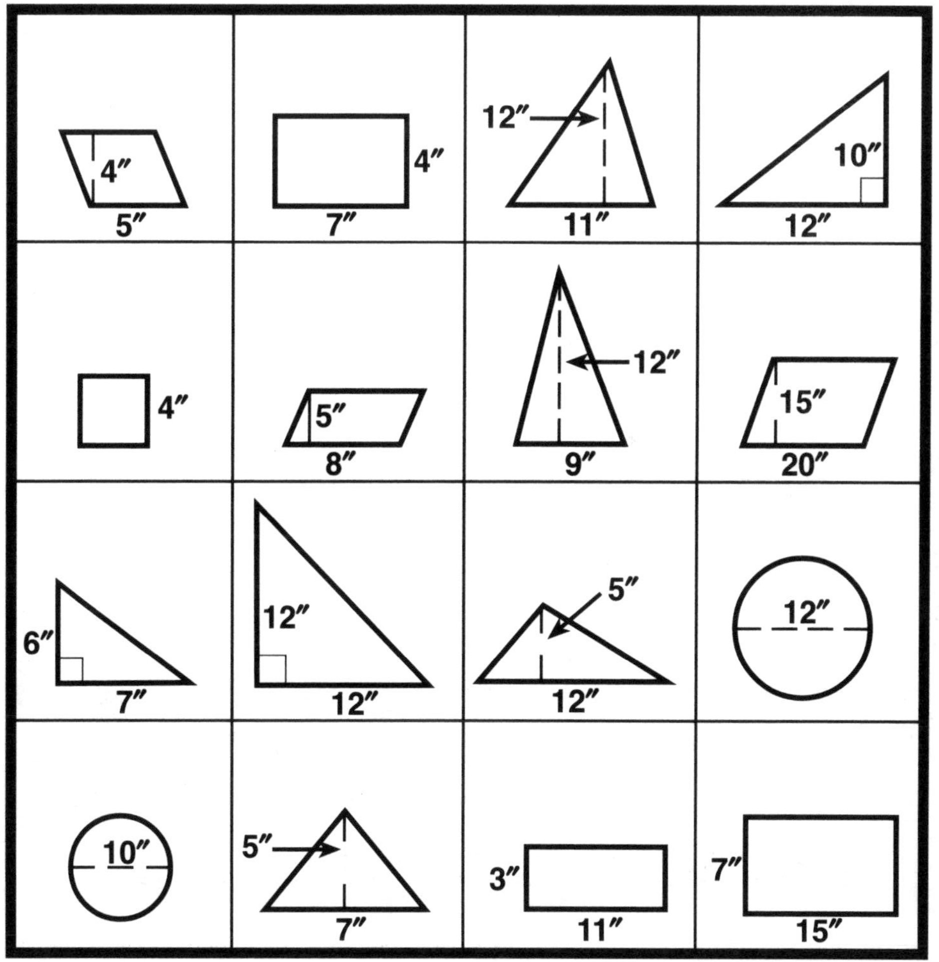

NCTM Standard: Geometry – analyze properties of two-dimensional shapes

Match the definitions below with the answers in the boxes to the right.

1. A shape with 4 congruent sides and 4 right angles
2. A shape with 4 sides, with the opposite sides parallel and equal
3. A shape with 3 sides
4. A specific place in space
5. A shape with 3 congruent sides
6. Lines in the same plane that never cross
7. An angle inside of a polygon
8. A shape with 2 pairs of parallel lines and 4 congruent sides
9. A triangle with 2 congruent sides
10. A triangle with no congruent sides
11. A quadrilateral with one pair of parallel lines
12. A shape with 2 pairs of parallel lines, 4 right angles, and 2 pairs of congruent sides
13. A triangle with one 90° angle
14. An angle larger than 90°
15. When 2 angles add up to 90°
16. When the sum of 2 angles is 180°

Search for the Geometric Gold

isosceles	complementary angles	triangle	supplementary angles
trapezoid	square	interior angle	right triangle
equilateral triangle	scalene	parallel lines	parallelogram
rhombus	obtuse angle	point	rectangle

NCTM Standard: Geometry – describe, classify, and understand relationships among two- and three-dimensional objects, using defining properties such as surface area and volume

Volley for Volume

Determine the volume for each figure to the right, and then match the volumes below to the correct figures in the boxes to the right.

1. 90 cubic inches
2. 108 cubic inches
3. 2,250 cubic inches
4. 36 cubic inches
5. 140 cubic inches
6. 300 cubic inches
7. 30 cubic inches
8. 240 cubic inches
9. 144 cubic inches
10. 64 cubic inches
11. 440 cubic inches
12. 84 cubic inches
13. 200 cubic inches
14. 288 cubic inches
15. 168 cubic inches

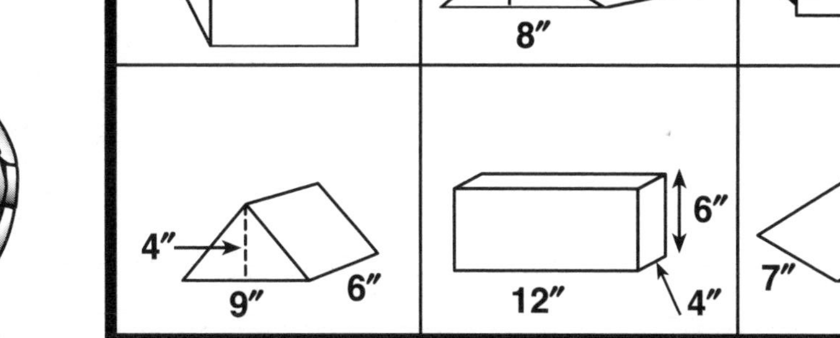

NCTM Standard: Geometry – describe, classify, and understand relationships among two- and three-dimensional objects, using defining properties such as surface area and volume

Wangle Surface Areas

Find the surface area of each figure to the right, and then match the surface areas below with the correct figures in the boxes to the right.

1. 132 square inches
2. 242 square inches
3. 198 square inches
4. 136 square inches
5. 208 square inches
6. 54 square inches
7. 400 square inches
8. 252 square inches
9. 72 square inches
10. 114 square inches
11. 333 square inches
12. 178 square inches
13. 68 square inches
14. 174 square inches
15. 172 square inches

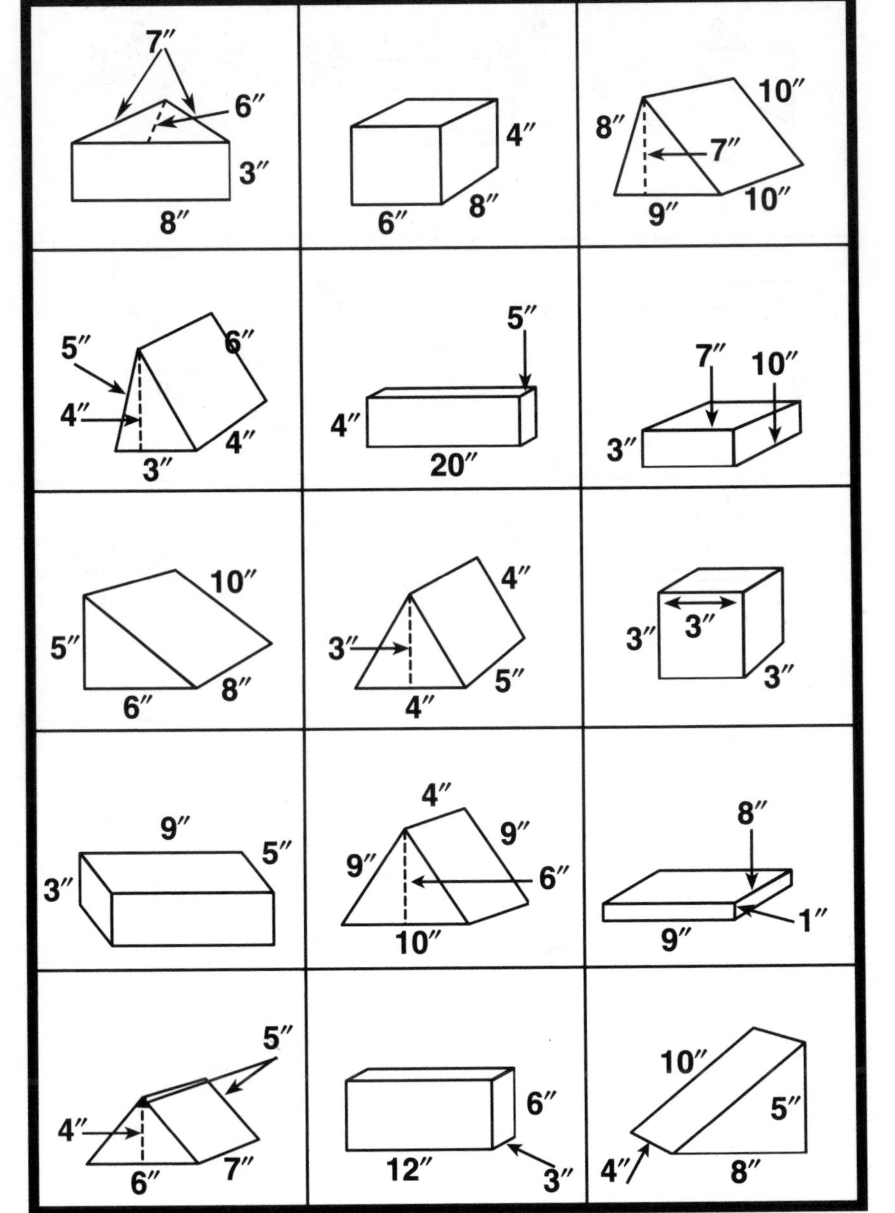

NCTM Standard: Measurement – understand both metric and customary systems of measurement

Use the inch ruler directly below to measure each of the long boxes beneath it, and then find the answer in the boxes to the right.

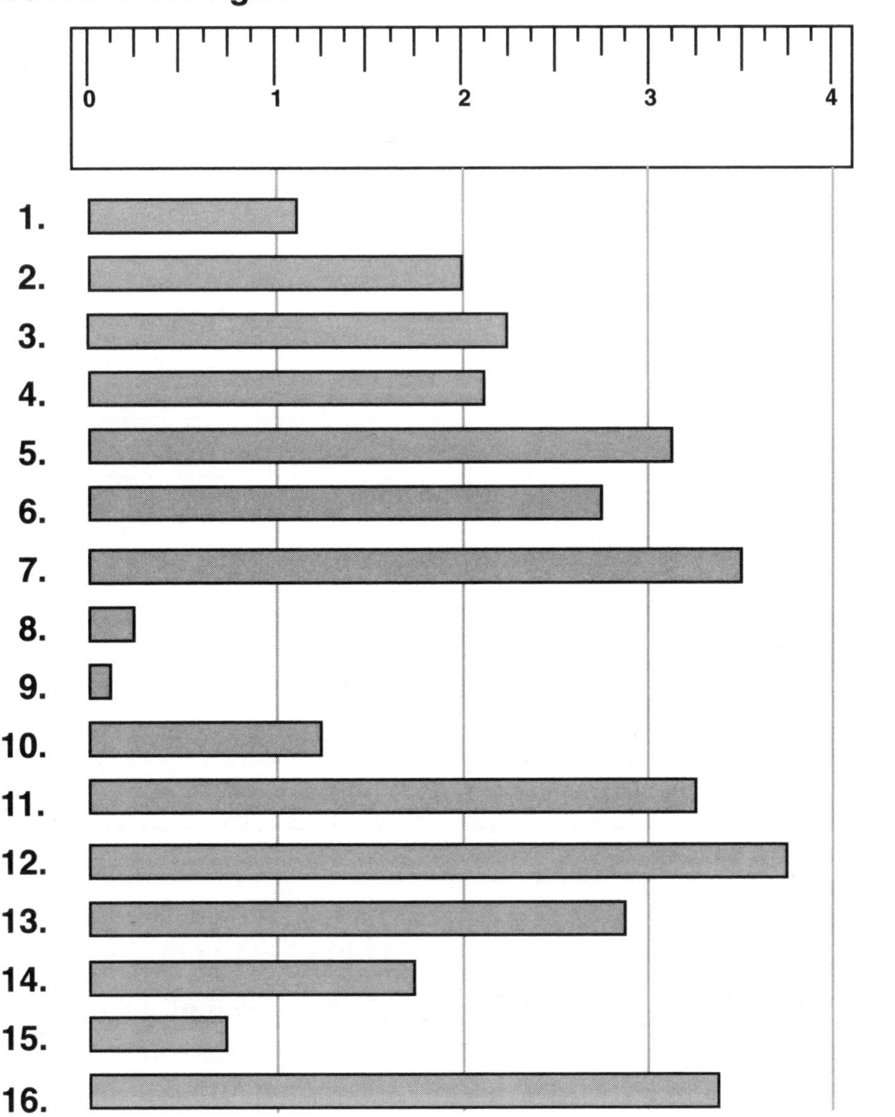

CRUNCH CUSTOMARY UNITS

CRUNCH

$3\frac{3}{4}''$	$2\frac{1}{4}''$	$3\frac{3}{8}''$	$\frac{1}{8}''$
$3\frac{1}{2}''$	$1\frac{3}{4}''$	$1\frac{1}{4}''$	$1\frac{1}{8}''$
$\frac{1}{4}''$	$2''$	$\frac{3}{4}''$	$3\frac{1}{8}''$
$2\frac{1}{8}''$	$2\frac{7}{8}''$	$2\frac{3}{4}''$	$3\frac{1}{4}''$

NCTM Standard: Measurement – understand both metric and customary systems of measurement

The ruler directly below represents metric measurement. Use it to measure each of the long boxes beneath it, and then find the answer in the boxes to the right.

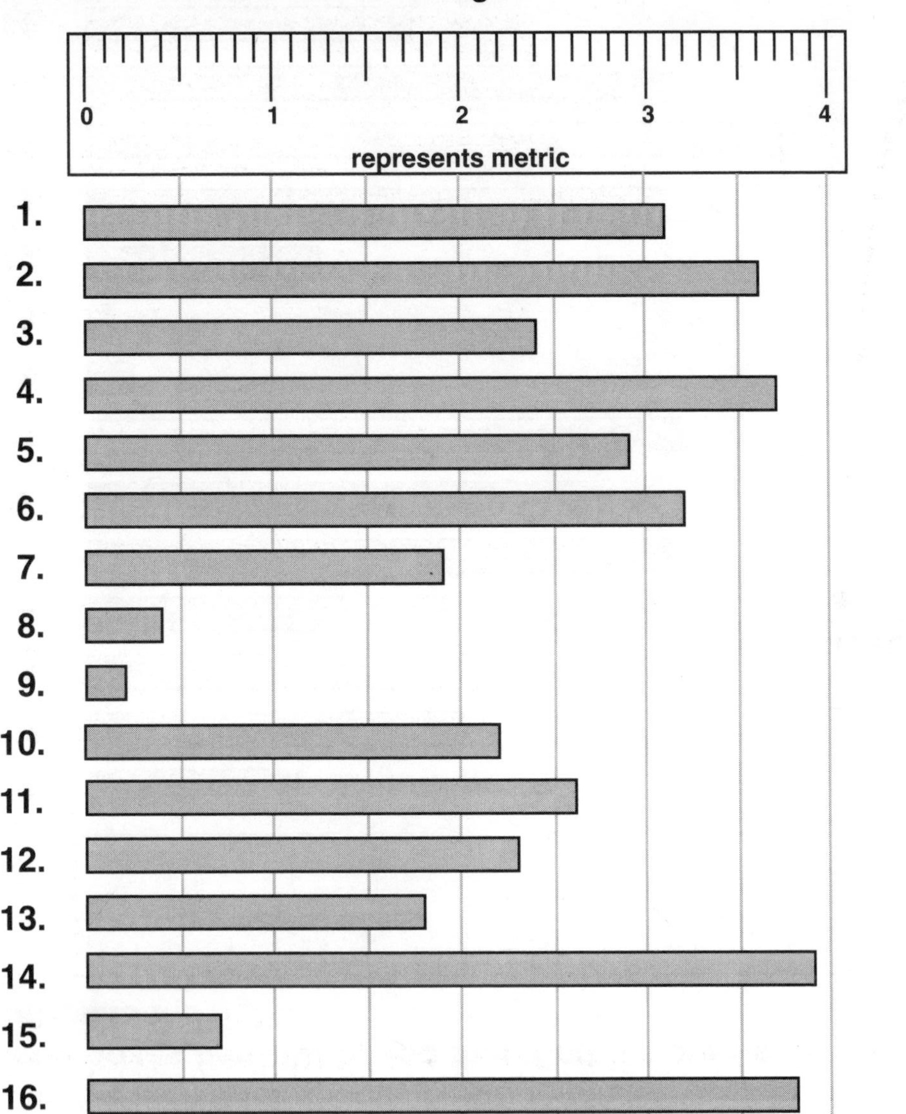

Munch Some Metrics

2.2 cm	3.9 cm	0.4 cm	1.9 cm
3.7 cm	1.8 cm	2.6 cm	3.1 cm
2.3 cm	3.2 cm	2.9 cm	0.7 cm
3.6 cm	0.2 cm	3.8 cm	2.4 cm

NCTM Standard: Measurement – understand both metric and customary systems of measurement

Use the inch ruler directly below to measure each of the long boxes beneath it, and then find the answer in the boxes to the right.

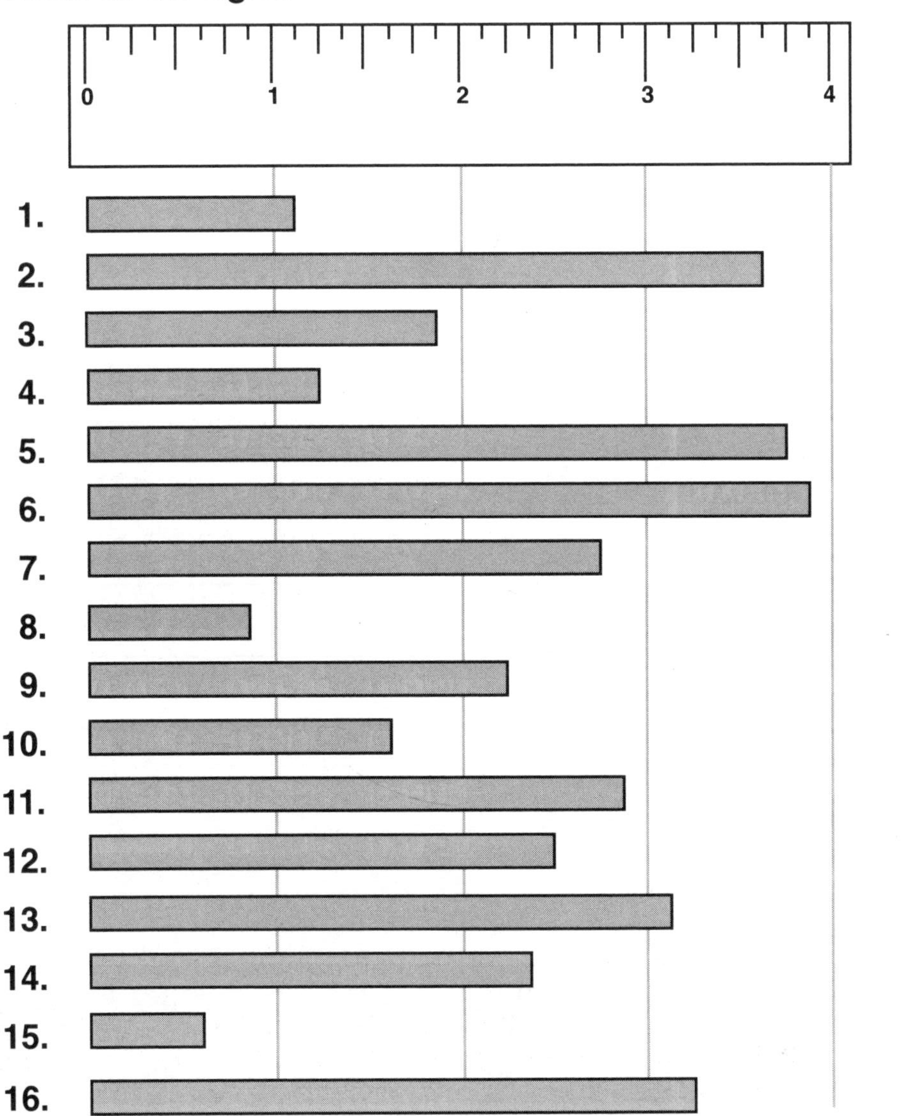

SWAP CUSTOMARY UNITS

$2\frac{7}{8}''$	$3\frac{1}{4}''$	$1\frac{7}{8}''$	$2\frac{1}{4}''$
$1\frac{1}{4}''$	$2\frac{3}{4}''$	$\frac{5}{8}''$	$3\frac{7}{8}''$
$1\frac{5}{8}''$	$2\frac{3}{8}''$	$1\frac{1}{8}''$	$2\frac{1}{2}''$
$3\frac{5}{8}''$	$\frac{7}{8}''$	$3\frac{1}{8}''$	$3\frac{3}{4}''$

NCTM Standard: Number and Operations – understand relationships among numbers

Douse the Density Property

The density property states that "between every two rational numbers, no matter how close, there is another rational number." For each item below, find the rational number that would be between the two rational numbers shown.

1. $\frac{1}{5}$ ↑ $\frac{2}{5}$
2. $\frac{1}{6}$ ↑ $\frac{2}{6}$
3. $\frac{3}{5}$ ↑ $\frac{4}{5}$
4. $2\frac{1}{8}$ ↑ $2\frac{2}{8}$
5. $3\frac{1}{3}$ ↑ $3\frac{2}{3}$
6. $1\frac{3}{5}$ ↑ $1\frac{4}{5}$
7. $5\frac{1}{7}$ ↑ $5\frac{2}{7}$
8. $\frac{5}{8}$ ↑ $\frac{6}{8}$
9. $\frac{3}{7}$ ↑ $\frac{4}{7}$
10. $\frac{5}{9}$ ↑ $\frac{6}{9}$
11. $\frac{1}{12}$ ↑ $\frac{2}{12}$
12. $1\frac{1}{4}$ ↑ $1\frac{1}{2}$
13. $\frac{1}{9}$ ↑ $\frac{2}{9}$
14. $3\frac{1}{6}$ ↑ $3\frac{2}{6}$
15. $2\frac{4}{9}$ ↑ $2\frac{5}{9}$

$3\frac{3}{12}$ or $3\frac{1}{4}$	$2\frac{9}{18}$ or $2\frac{1}{2}$	$1\frac{7}{10}$
$\frac{3}{10}$	$\frac{11}{18}$	$\frac{3}{18}$ or $\frac{1}{6}$
$5\frac{3}{14}$	$\frac{3}{12}$ or $\frac{1}{4}$	$2\frac{3}{16}$
$1\frac{3}{8}$	$\frac{3}{24}$ or $\frac{1}{8}$	$\frac{7}{14}$ or $\frac{1}{2}$
$3\frac{3}{6}$ or $3\frac{1}{2}$	$\frac{11}{16}$	$\frac{7}{10}$

NCTM Standard: Number and Operations – understand and use properties of operations such as the distributivity of multiplication over addition

DRAW IN THE DISTRIBUTIVE PROPERTY

Below are some problems showing the use of the distributive property. Find the easier solution to each in the boxes at the right.

1. 8 x 45 =
2. 6 x 57 =
3. 6 x 75 =
4. 8 x 54 =
5. 5 x 84 =
6. 6 x 54 =
7. 7 x 75 =
8. 5 x 48 =
9. 6 x 45 =
10. 7 x 57 =
11. 8 x 35 =
12. 7 x 54 =
13. 8 x 53 =
14. 7 x 35 =
15. 7 x 45 =

(6 x 40) + (6 x 5)	(8 x 50) + (8 x 3)	(7 x 50) + (7 x 4)
(8 x 30) + (8 x 5)	(6 x 50) + (6 x 7)	(7 x 50) + (7 x 7)
(8 x 50) + (8 x 4)	(7 x 40) + (7 x 5)	(7 x 70) + (7 x 5)
(7 x 30) + (7 x 5)	(5 x 80) + (5 x 4)	(6 x 70) + (6 x 5)
(8 x 40) + (8 x 5)	(5 x 40) + (5 x 8)	(6 x 50) + (6 x 4)

NCTM Standard: Geometry – analyze properties of two-dimensional geometric shapes; understand transformations

Grapple Geometric Patterns

In each item below is a series of geometric shapes. Find the next shape that would be in each pattern from the shapes in the boxes at the right.

1. ____________________
2. ____________________
3. ____________________
4. ____________________
5. ____________________
6. ____________________
7. ____________________
8. ____________________
9. ____________________
10. ____________________
11. ____________________
12. ____________________
13. ____________________
14. ____________________
15. ____________________
16. ____________________

NCTM Standard: Geometry – apply transformations and use of symmetry to analyze mathematical situations

Pack Away Patterns

Study each pattern below, and find the shape that would come next in each pattern from the shapes in the boxes at the right.

1.
2.
3.
4.
5.
6.
7.
8.
9.
10.
11.
12.
13.
14.
15.

NCTM Standard: Number and Operations – understand relationships among numbers

Pick Up a Numerical Pattern

22 27 32 37 42 47

Determine the numerical pattern in each problem below. Then find the number that would come next in the pattern in the boxes at the right.

1. 545; 550; 555; 560; ...
2. 5,545; 5,550; 5,555; ...
3. 5,565; 5,560; 5,555; ...
4. 575; 571; 567; 563; ...
5. 5,700; 5,750; 5,800; 5,850; ...
6. 5,999; 5,991; 5,983; 5,975; ...
7. 576; 567; 558; 549; 540; ...
8. 576; 569; 562; 555; 548; ...
9. -45; -43; -41; -39; -37; ...
10. -31; -34; -37; -40; -43; ...
11. -51; -46; -42; -39; -37; ...
12. 521; 541; 561; 581; 601; ...
13. 632; 621; 610; 599; 588; ...
14. -521; -523; -525; -527; ...
15. -521; -518; -515; -512; ...
16. 568; 572; 577; 583; 590; ...

621	-46	-529	5,900
5,560	-509	577	-36
559	-35	565	531
5,967	541	598	5,550

NCTM Standard: Number and Operations – understand ways of representing numbers and work flexibly with fractions, decimals, and percents

You are all familiar with store sales. Below are some items that have been reduced in a store. Find out how much money would be taken off of each item, and then find the answers in the boxes at the right.

1. 30% off of $300.00
2. 25% off of $70.00
3. 40% off of $50.00
4. 35% off of $2,500.00
5. 25% off of $25.00
6. 20% off of $80.00
7. 25% off of $200.00
8. 75% off of $500.00
9. 75% off of $30.00
10. 25% off of $700.00
11. 20% off of $700.00
12. 25% off of $60.00
13. 25% off of $40.00
14. 35% off of $300.00
15. 40% off of $70.00
16. 20% off of $8,000.00

Snare Sale Prices

$16	$20	$105	$22.50
$140	$375	$1,600	$6.25
$875	$10	$17.50	$15
$90	$175	$28	$50

NCTM Standard: Number and Operations – compute fluently; work flexibly with percents to solve problems; make reasonable estimates

TAG THE PERCENT ONE NUMBER IS OF ANOTHER NUMBER

Solve the problems below, and find the answers in the boxes at the right.

1. What percent is 1 of 100?
2. What percent is 2 of 100?
3. What percent is 8 of 200?
4. What percent is 10 of 50?
5. What percent is 2 of 2?
6. What percent is 20 of 40?
7. What percent is 65 of 100?
8. What percent is 10 of 40?
9. What percent is 98 of 100?
10. What percent is 2 of 20?
11. What percent is 30 of 500?
12. What percent is 3 of 100?
13. What percent is 12 of 10?
14. What percent is 4 of 5?
15. What percent is 6 of 8?
16. What percent is 9 of 10?

10%
65%
4%
3%
20%

98%	50%	6%	90%
25%	2%	120%	100%
4%	80%	1%	10%
75%	20%	65%	3%

NCTM Standard: Number and Operations – understand ways of representing numbers and work flexibly with fractions, decimals, and percents

Below is a chart showing hourly, daily, weekly, or monthly wage. In the second column, it shows the percent increase in the salary the person will receive. Find the resulting wage after the increase in the boxes at the right.

Wage	Percent Increase
1. $5.00 per hour	2%
2. $200.00 per week	3%
3. $200.00 per month	10%
4. $500.00 per month	8%
5. $7.00 per hour	3%
6. $40.00 per day	6%
7. $300.00 per week	10%
8. $300.00 per month	5%
9. $200.00 per month	15%
10. $10.00 per hour	2%
11. $400.00 per week	5%
12. $400.00 per month	12%
13. $500.00 per week	6%
14. $20.00 per hour	8%
15. $400.00 per month	15%
16. $600.00 per month	10%

Wrap Up a Raise

$530	$10.20	$42.40	$660
$540	$460	$220	$21.60
$315	$5.10	$330	$420
$230	$206	$7.21	$448

NCTM Standard: Number and Operations – compute fluently and make reasonable estimates

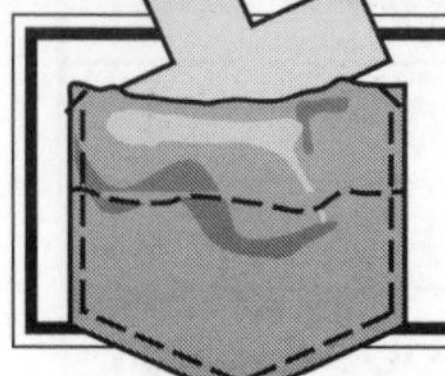

POCKET POSITIVE AND NEGATIVE SOLUTIONS

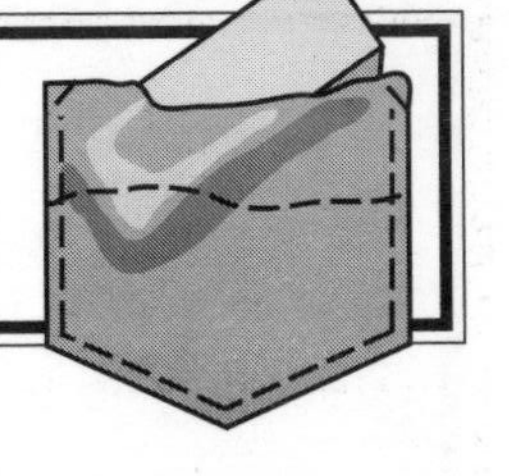

Find the solution to each of the addition problems below in the boxes at the right.

1. -35 + -61 =
2. +56 + -23 =
3. +43 + -73 =
4. -45 + +22 =
5. +56 + -21 =
6. -102 + -32 =
7. +23 + -35 =
8. +34 + -56 =
9. +109 + -73 =
10. +21 + -10 =
11. +62 + -93 =
12. -38 + -21 =
13. -30 + -90 =
14. +21 + -21 =
15. -20 + +40 =
16. +32 + -43 =

+35	**+36**	**-12**	**-30**
-23	**-31**	**-11**	**-120**
-22	**-134**	**0**	**+33**
-96	**-59**	**+20**	**+11**

NCTM Standard: Number and Operations – understand relationships among numbers

Rack Up Some Positive and Negative Numbers

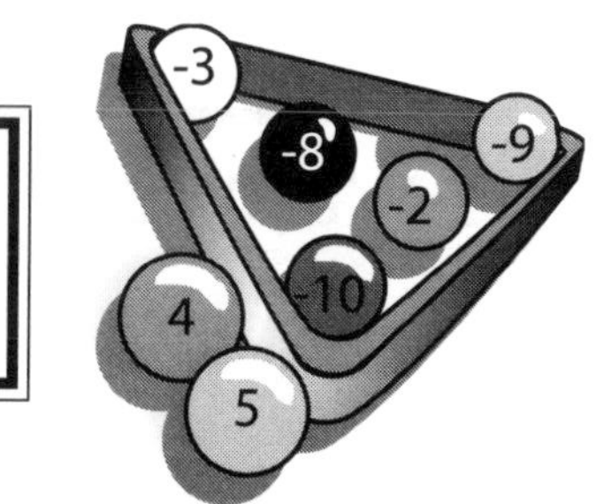

Determine the number represented by the arrow on each number line. Find the answers in the boxes at the right.

-3	-15	-19
4	5	-16
-18	-1	-10
-14	-5	-9
-2	0	-8

NCTM Standard: Number and Operations – understand the place-value structure of the base ten system

Determine the large number represented by the dots in each place below, and find the matching number in the boxes at the right.

	millions				thousands				ones		
	H	T	O		H	T	O		H	T	O
1.	•••	•	••		•	••	•		•••		••••
2.	•••		•••		•		•		•••		••
3.	•••	•	•		•	••	•		•••		•
4.	•••	•	•		•	•••	•		•••	••	•
5.	•••	••	•		•	•••	•		•••	•	•
6.	•••	•	•••		••	•	•••		••	•	•••
7.	•	•••	•••		•••						•••••
8.	•	•••	•••			•	••		•	•••	•••••
9.	•	•••	•			•	•••		•	•••	•••••
10.	•	•••	•		•••	•	•••		•••	•••	•••
11.	•	•••	•		•••	•			•••		••
12.	•	•••	•		•••	•			•••	•••	•••••

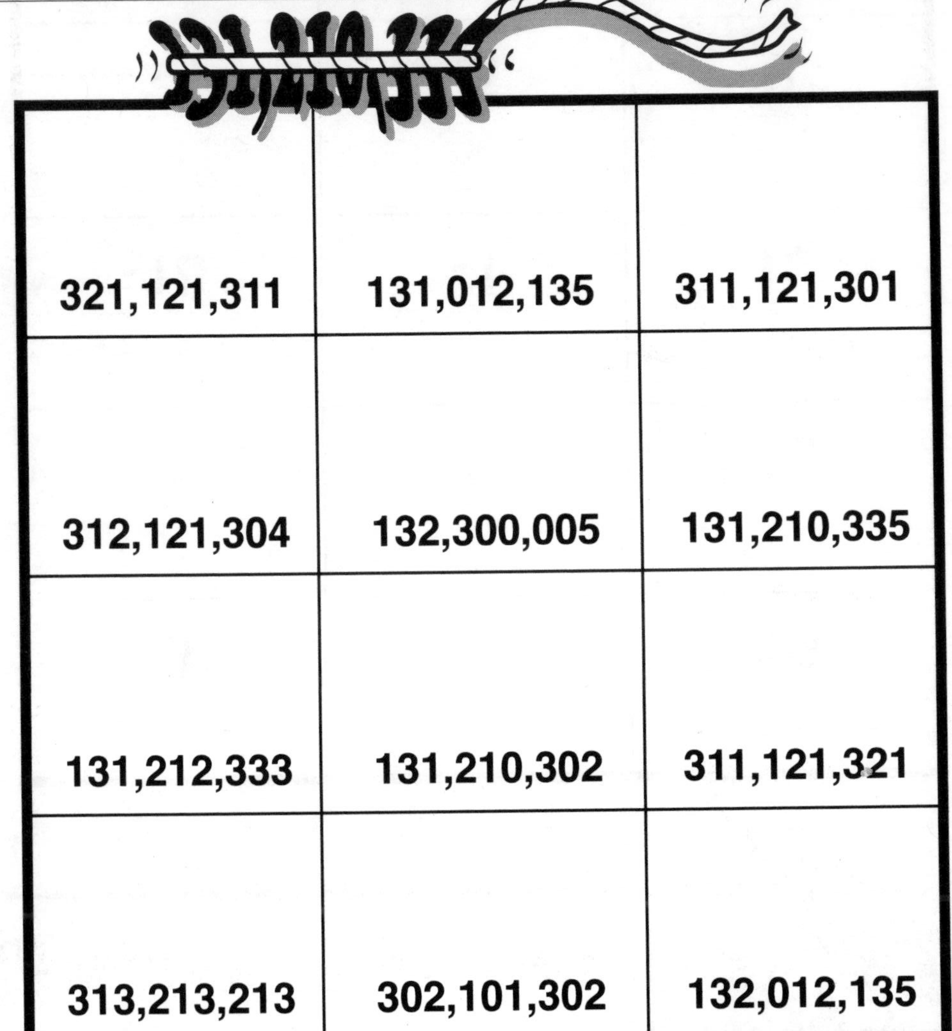

321,121,311	131,012,135	311,121,301
312,121,304	132,300,005	131,210,335
131,212,333	131,210,302	311,121,321
313,213,213	302,101,302	132,012,135

NCTM Standard: Number and Operations – understand the place-value structure of the base ten system

Determine the large number represented by the dots in each place below, and find the matching number in the boxes at the right.

MASTER HUGE NUMBERS

	billions			millions			thousands			ones		
	H	T	O	H	T	O	H	T	O	H	T	O
1.				••	•			•		•		
2.			•									
3.			•			•						
4.				•	•				•			
5.					•	•						
6.						•		•			•	
7.							•	•				
8.						•	•				••	•
9.										•		
10.				••		•	•		•		•	
11.					•		•					
12.				•								
13.			•		•		•					
14.						•						
15.							•	•		•		
16.					•	••	•					

201,101,010	1,100,021	12,100,000	1,010,010
1,010,100,000	210,010,100	1,000,000,000	100,000,000
1,001,000,000	110,100	100	11,000,000
110,000	110,001,000	10,100,000	1,000,000

NCTM Standard: Number and Operations – understand the place-value structure of the base ten system

Roll in Tricky Place Value

Determine the number represented by each item below, and find the answer in the boxes at the right.

1. 56 tens, 20 hundreds, 2 ones
2. 56 hundreds, 3 ones, 2 tens
3. 6 tens, 56 hundreds, 2 ones
4. 56 hundreds, 20 tens, 3 ones
5. 20 tens, 61 ones, 3 hundreds
6. 20 tens, 61 hundreds, 3 ones
7. 61 hundreds, 20 ones, 3 tens
8. 61 hundreds, 3 ones, 2 tens
9. 20 hundreds, 3 tens, 20 ones
10. 50 tens, 2 hundreds, 49 ones
11. 49 tens, 50 hundreds, 3 ones
12. 49 hundreds, 3 tens, 50 ones
13. 49 ones, 0 tens, 49 hundreds
14. 49 ones, 5 tens, 50 hundreds
15. 20 hundreds, 30 tens, 2 ones
16. 40 tens, 53 hundreds, 2 ones

5,662	749	5,803	4,949
2,050	6,303	2,302	6,150
4,980	5,623	6,123	5,702
2,562	5,099	561	5,493

NCTM Standard: Number and Operations – understand the place-value structure of the base ten system

WANGLE SOME BIG WHOLE NUMBERS

Rearrange the numbers in each item below to make the greatest number possible. Find that number in the boxes at the right.

1. 5 6 0 3 1
2. 7 8 9 9 0
3. 1 0 8 3 2
4. 8 1 0 2 9
5. 9 2 1 9 9
6. 1 0 8 5 3
7. 0 1 0 2 8
8. 2 8 8 1 1
9. 8 7 9 1 0
10. 9 1 0 2 3
11. 1 2 0 1 2
12. 0 2 1 1 1
13. 0 0 0 1 0
14. 0 0 1 2 1
15. 7 8 9 9 1
16. 2 5 1 1 2

88,211	99,921	52,211	98,710
99,871	65,310	21,110	85,310
99,870	93,210	98,210	10,000
82,100	21,100	83,210	22,110

Answer Keys

***Only the problem numbers are included in the boxes. It is recommended to write the correct problem numbers on a full-size copy of each math game page to create an answer key.**

Dance Away With Algebraic Expressions (p. 3)

6	15	9
11	1	13
4	12	3
2	10	7
8	5	14

Glide Through Algebraic Equations (p. 4)

14	4	15	3
10	11	16	2
8	7	12	9
1	13	6	5

Hook Algebraic Unknowns (p. 5)

16	1	15	12
6	14	2	8
7	3	9	11
5	13	4	10

Zip Away With Algebraic Expressions (p. 6)

9	1	16	11
6	12	13	5
14	2	8	10
4	7	15	3

Grip Some Graphing (p. 7)

6	11	4
5	14	10
13	1	7
8	9	12
3	15	2

Lap Up Laps (p. 8)

10	3	12
4	8	1
2	13	5
15	6	9
7	14	11

Earn Some Decimals (p. 9)

16	4	15	8
12	7	2	13
1	6	9	10
3	11	14	5

Get Ready to Nab Decimals on a Number Line (p. 10)

14	7	3
15	1	13
9	11	5
2	8	10
6	12	4

Rack Up Rounding Decimals to the Thousandths (p. 11)

1	8	14
9	7	12
3	11	4
5	10	15
6	2	13

Reap Rounding Decimals to the Hundredths (p. 12)

2	13	7
14	1	15
8	12	10
4	11	3
6	9	5

Slam Dunk Some Decimal Ordering (p. 13)

11	8	4
1	15	13
14	5	10
9	3	12
6	7	2

Swap Some Decimal Values (p. 14)

14	2	7
9	5	13
3	12	6
15	10	4
1	8	11

Sweep Up Decimals (p. 15)

9	1	6
3	7	11
10	4	12
8	2	5

Swoop Up Rounding Decimals (p. 16)

5	1	13
8	12	2
3	15	11
10	14	9
6	4	7

Tag Some Ordered Decimals (p. 17)

5	12	10
14	8	4
1	15	7
11	3	13
6	9	2

Ambush Some Decimal Round-ups (p. 18)

14	1	15	9
7	11	3	16
2	8	13	5
6	12	4	10

Dive for Decimal Quotient Unknowns (p. 19)

11	3	12
6	13	5
9	7	4
2	15	10
14	8	1

Extract Some Decimal Division Estimations (p. 20)

11	1	4
2	13	10
14	3	8
5	7	15
9	12	6

Groove With Decimal Multiples (p. 21)

14	6	2
13	12	10
4	1	8
7	11	5
3	9	15

Dive Into Challenging Division (p. 22)

2	11	15	12
6	4	8	9
3	13	16	5
7	14	10	1

Pounce on Proportions (p. 23)

3	8	11
9	14	7
12	2	15
6	13	5
4	10	1

Search for a Square Root (p. 24)

15	9	14
12	4	1
10	2	5
11	7	8
6	3	13

Strike Out Square Roots (p. 25)

10	5	14
6	2	15
8	12	3
1	9	13
7	4	11

Bring in a Flood of Quotients (p. 26)

4	11	12	3
13	16	8	7
15	2	6	14
1	9	10	5

Conquer Multiplying Mixed Numbers (p. 27)

9	10	4	5
3	15	2	13
6	1	16	8
11	14	7	12

Finding Fractional Parts of Whole Numbers (p. 28)

10	7	16	11
3	1	12	5
4	15	2	9
13	8	14	6

Grasp a Fractional Location (p. 29)

5	11	12	4
15	3	8	9
13	7	2	16
1	10	14	6

Lock Onto a Fraction (p. 30)

16	12	7	2
1	15	9	11
5	4	13	8
10	14	6	3

Win a Product (p. 31)

8	15	2
14	6	13
11	1	7
12	5	10
4	9	3

Finding Fraction-Decimal Equivalents (p. 32)

4	9	12
6	11	2
3	7	14
13	1	15
8	5	10

Grab on to Fraction-Decimal-Percent Equivalents (p. 33)

10	8	5	3
4	11	13	1
12	14	6	15
2	9	16	7

Buffalo Some Triangular Perimeters (p. 34)

3	10	1
14	5	6
13	9	11
7	4	2
15	12	8

Dive Into Triangular Areas (p. 35)

6	12	7
15	1	14
11	13	10
4	3	2
8	9	5

Fetch Figures in Space (p. 36)

12	2	1
11	9	5
6	3	8
7	4	10

Grab a Coordinate (p. 37)

12	19	3	14
16	2	22	6
7	18	11	1
17	13	20	15
4	24	10	23
21	9	5	8

Lasso Lines and Points (p. 38)

8	13	15	3
9	1	11	2
5	6	12	16
7	4	14	10

Latch on to Two-Dimensional Areas (p. 39)

7	10	6	13
14	8	12	9
15	1	5	11
2	3	16	4

Search for the Geometric Gold (p. 40)

9	15	3	16
11	1	7	13
5	10	6	2
8	14	4	12

Volley for Volume (p. 41)

3	6	15
7	8	13
4	11	10
1	12	9
2	14	5

Wangle Surface Areas (p. 42)

10	5	11
13	7	2
3	9	6
14	15	12
4	8	1

Crush Customary Units (p. 43)

12	3	16	9
7	14	10	1
8	2	15	5
4	13	6	11

Munch Some Metrics (p. 44)

10	14	8	7
4	13	11	1
12	6	5	15
2	9	16	3

Swap Customary Units (p. 45)

11	16	3	9
4	7	15	6
10	14	1	12
2	8	13	5

Douse the Density Property (p. 46)

14	15	6
1	10	13
7	2	4
12	11	9
5	8	3

Draw in the Distributive Property (p. 47)

9	13	12
11	2	10
4	15	7
14	5	3
1	8	6

Grapple Geometric Patterns (p. 48)

8	7	1	4
5	3	2	15
6	11	13	16
10	12	14	9

Pack Away Patterns (p. 49)

5	3	15
1	14	6
2	7	13
9	10	12
8	11	4

Pick Up a Numerical Pattern (p. 50)

12	10	14	5
2	15	13	11
4	9	1	7
6	8	16	3

Snare Sale Prices (p. 51)

6	3	14	9
11	8	16	5
4	13	2	12
1	10	15	7

Tag the Percent One Number Is of Another Number (p. 52)

9	6	11	16
8	2	13	5
3	14	1	10
15	4	7	12

Wrap Up a Raise (p. 53)

13	10	6	16
4	15	3	14
8	1	7	11
9	2	5	12

Pocket Positive and Negative Solutions (p. 54)

5	9	7	3
4	11	16	13
8	6	14	2
1	12	15	10

Rack Up Some Positive and Negative Numbers (p. 55)

8	13	3
10	11	5
2	1	14
6	9	7
4	15	12

Ensnare Some Big Numbers (p. 56)

5	9	3
1	7	12
10	11	4
6	2	8

Master Huge Numbers (p. 57)

10	8	16	6
13	1	2	12
3	15	9	5
7	4	11	14

Roll in Tricky Place Value (p. 58)

3	10	4	13
9	6	15	7
12	2	8	16
1	14	5	11

Wangle Some Big Whole Numbers (p. 59)

8	5	16	9
15	1	12	6
2	10	4	13
7	14	3	11